HADRIAN'S WALL

Edge of an Empire

Over the heather the wet wind blows
I've lice in my tunic and a cold in my nose.

The rain comes pattering out of the sky
I'm a Wall soldier, and I don't know why.

W.H. Auden: *Roman Wall Blues*

Looking to the Great Whin Sill.

HADRIAN'S WALL

Edge of an Empire

ED GELDARD

The Crowood Press

First published in 2011 by
The Crowood Press Ltd
Ramsbury, Marlborough
Wiltshire SN8 2HR

www.crowood.com

British Library Cataloguing-in-Publication Data
A catalogue record for this book is available from the British Library.

ISBN 978 1 84797 273 6

Acknowledgements
This book could not have been written without the help of a number of people who, with no thought of reward, gave up their free time to help me. I should like to take this opportunity to thank Tyne & Wear Museums; Andrew Parkin of The Society of Antiquaries, Newcastle-upon-Tyne; Tim Padley of Tullie House; Robin Birley; English Heritage; Gary Craven; Lynn Pope; Dr Desmond Walker (Retd); John Conyard of Comitatus, York; Mark & Jill Hatch of the Roman Military Research Society at Colchester; Paul Carrick of Cohors V Gaul at Arbeia Roman Fort, South Shields; Gordon Henderson of VII Claudia group at Binchester Fort; Robin Brown of Legio VIII Augusta MGV; The Ermine Street Guard; Steve Richardson and the Tyne Team; Alex Croom for the information on food; and the staff of Spennymoor Library. All have played a part in the making of this book. Every effort has been made to ensure the accuracy of the information within; any errors are mine.

   My greatest debt in writing this book is to my partner Maggie; her unfailing good advice guided me all the way.

Typeset by Jean Cussons Typesetting, Diss, Norfolk

Printed and bound in China by Everbest Printing Co. Ltd

CONTENTS

INTRODUCTION

Hadrian's Wall, built under the keen eye of Aulus Platorius Nepos, governor of Roman Britain, on the orders of the Emperor Hadrian, is now a peaceful place, but this was not always so. Almost since its creation it has been a source of fascination, attracting visitors from all walks of life. From the personal odyssey of William Hutton who examined, in 'minute detail', its entire length, to the social excursions of the Society of Antiquaries, the visitor experience of the Wall has been diverse.

Running through some of the most scenic landscape in Britain, Hadrian's Wall was the most formidable of fortifications: a wall that stretched from coast to coast in a hostile land. What stands today is a reminder of the power and limits of an empire the Romans had taken 1,200 years to build. Like the Great Wall of China, it disregards hills and valleys, at times choosing what seems to be the most difficult route. Unlike the Great Wall, it has suffered badly at the hands of stone robbers. Much of Hadrian's Wall has now disappeared; what remains was due to the efforts of a Newcastle lawyer named John Clayton who, in order to preserve it, bought up much of the land on which it stood. Today few people have heard of John Clayton and yet he is one of the most important individuals in the history of the Wall. His fascination with Roman relics prompted him to purchase long sections of the Wall, which saw the first of many excavations; and it was his enthusiasm that helped preserve the best sections of the wall. A painting at Wallington Hall in Northumberland shows a centurion supervising the building of the wall; the centurion's face is that of John Clayton.

It was William Hutton, an archaeologist from Birmingham, who first sowed the seeds of the idea for this walk more than a century ago. On 14 July 1801, at the age of seventy-eight, he set out from Birmingham 'to see a shattered Wall'. Hutton tells us:

> I was dressed in black, a kind of religious travelling warrant, but divested of assuming airs; and had a black pouch much like a postman's letter pouch in which were deposited the maps of Cumberland, Northumberland and the Wall, with its appendages; all three taken out of Gough's edition of the *Camden's Britannica*. To this little 'pocket' I fastened an umbrella in a green case, for I was not likely to have a six weeks' tour without wet, and flung it over that shoulder which was the least tired.

On reaching Carlisle he went on to walk the Wall in both directions in seven days and six hours. By the time he returned to Birmingham on 7 August he had walked 601 miles (967km), lost 1 stone (6kg) in weight and spent forty guineas. At times he was walking up to 28 miles (45km) in a day. He concluded by saying 'I could travel the Wall a third time, with the expense only of a few shillings.' In his book *The History of the Roman Wall* he wrote 'Perhaps I am the first man who ever travelled the whole length of the Wall and probably the last one who will ever attempt it.'

How wrong he was. On 23 May 2003, the only National Trail within a Heritage Site was opened; it was called Hadrian's Wall Path.

Ed Geldard

CHAPTER I

HADRIAN: THE MAN

Our own constitution was the product not of one genius but of many; it was not established within the lifetime of one man but was the work of several men in several generations.

Cato (234–149BC)

To understand the background of Publius Aelius Hadrianus – the Emperor Hadrian – we must look back more than two centuries from his birth, to 151BC. Carthage was at war with Rome, and for a time the war went against the Romans; however, after a year of desperate fighting Scipio Aemilianus, then a subordinate officer, took on the role of consul in order to hold supreme command. The Senate ordered him to raze Carthage to the ground, and although he dutifully carried out the will of the Senate what he had done filled him with remorse. He was a man of culture and refinement; he spoke pure Latin and enjoyed intellectual conversation with Greek historians and poets. On his return to Rome he left behind the veterans, sick and wounded to re-establish the colonization of Spain; a programme that had been started by his grandfather sixty years earlier. Spain had become the richest possession of the Roman Empire; it produced gold, silver, lead and tin, and its olive oil was better even than that of Italy. Scipio's veterans, with their fighting days over, went on to marry local women and build small towns. One of these, in modern-day Andalusia in southern Spain, was Italica, so called to commemorate the motherland that they would never see again.

Hadrian was born in Italica on 24 January AD76. This is a fact affirmed in his imperial horoscope and has also been confirmed by various learned scholars who studied the life of Hadrian. However, the birth was erroneously assigned to Rome to give the appearance of Hadrian being pure-bred Roman instead of from the provinces. His given name was Publius and his family name Aelius. The third name, Hadrianus, meant he was of Hadria; that is, from the town of Hadria on the north-east coast of Italy in the district of Picenum. It was from there, almost three centuries before, that his forbears had arrived in Spain.

Bust of Hadrian.

No one could have foreseen that one day he would become emperor. However, when Hadrian was nine his father died and a distant relative, Trajan, took over his guardianship. Trajan, a successful general in this age of conflict, was also the adopted son of the childless emperor Nerva; he had been informed of his adoption in a handwritten note received from Nerva in AD97!

Trajan's early attempts to carve a military career for the young Hadrian were frustrated by the boy's liking for the easy life: he preferred hunting to that of army life. His first posting to Upper Germany as a military tribune (staff officer) ended with little distinction and Trajan recalled him to Rome so that he could keep a close eye on him. He then went on to serve as a tribune with Legio II Adiutrix before transferring to Legio V Minervia in Germany. Following the death of Nerva in AD98, Trajan became the new emperor and in one fell swoop transformed the lives of those around him, including Hadrian. The following seventeen years were to be some of the greatest in Rome's history, and it was in those seventeen years that Hadrian matured from being a youth to a man. In AD100 he married Trajan's great niece Vibia Sabina; this was to bring him ever closer to the childless emperor.

By this time Trajan had embarked on a series of wars to extend the Roman Empire. In the Balkans he defeated the Dacians, whose unruly borders were a constant thorn in the side of Rome. Hadrian served with distinction in both campaigns, and in the second Trajan was to present him with a valuable ring that at one time had belonged to Nerva; this appeared to designate Hadrian as his successor. He was an experienced officer who had served with three different legions. Trajan then annexed Armenia, declared war on the Parthians and invaded Mesopotamia (modern-day Iraq) to add new provinces to the empire. A sudden illness forced Trajan to return to Rome leaving Hadrian in charge of the army as well as the new province, so once again he found himself in a key post of the ever-growing empire. There was no doubt of Hadrian's standing now, and yet there were no immediate signs that Trajan intended to make him his imperial heir.

The details surrounding Hadrian's accession are something of a mystery. While he may have been the obvious choice, he had never actually been adopted as Trajan's heir. As he lay on his deathbed, nursed by his wife Plotina, Trajan may well have decided to do so but the sequence of events makes one suspicious. On 8 August 117 Trajan died at Selinus. It was announced at Antioch on the 9th that he had adopted Hadrian, but since Plotina signed the document herself it is thought that Trajan was already dead. It was only two days later, on the 11th, that Trajan's death was made known to the public. Hadrian's succession was, according to Cassius Dio, solely due to the actions of Plotina, for it was she who had for two days sent letters to the senate declaring Hadrian to be the new heir. Later,

when the papers of adoption were presented to the Senate they were at once endorsed, even though they looked suspiciously falsified. While Trajan may have shown Hadrian clear signs of favour he had never formally made him the heir apparent. On the contrary, Trajan had said that if he were to die there were a number of successors worthy of the title of Caesar. However, it was Publius Aelius Hadrianus who assumed the mantle of emperor.

Hadrian soon realized that he faced an empire in turmoil: he was to abandon the conquests of Trajan and withdraw the Roman army from all the territories beyond the Euphrates. In doing this he was following the advice set out a century earlier by Caesar Augustus, who had advised any successor to keep the empire within the natural boundaries of the rivers Rhine, Danube and Euphrates. This withdrawal did not make Hadrian popular; the Roman army had paid dearly in blood for this land. At first Hadrian did not go to Rome: he had to suppress a Jewish revolt that had broken out under Trajan, and then moved on to the Danube frontier to clear things there.

Whilst still in Dacia he received news of a plot against his life. Four leading Senators had been accused of conspiring against him and were put to death on orders from the Senate, hunted down and killed without a trial. If Hadrian had hoped to rule as honourably as his predecessor, then he had got off to a bad start – he was still on his way to Rome and four respected Senators were already dead. Many saw their deaths as the removal of all contenders to his throne as all four had been friends of Trajan and one of them, Gaius Nigrinus, was so influential that he was thought of as being the successor to Trajan. Despite Hadrian denying complicity in their deaths and firmly placing the blame on the shoulders of Attianus, prefect of the Praetorian Guard and his one-time joint guardian, a shadow was cast over his relations with the Senate for much of his reign. To appease the people of Rome he held games and shows; in addition all tax arrears for past years were cancelled and the bonds burned in the Forum of Trajan. Hadrian then went on to instigate far-reaching reforms, including that of Trajan's scheme for the 'alimentation' of poor children, but on a far larger scale.

Hadrian had come to the throne at the age of forty-one, having spent half of his life outside Italy. He was now to spend more than half of his reign travelling the empire implementing his policies in person. Hadrian's first great tour came in 121 when he travelled north to inspect the Germanic provinces on the Rhine. From here, he travelled to Britannia to quell a rebellion that had been going on for the past two years. He arrived in the spring of 122 and saw for himself the problems facing the territories; it was then that he initiated the building of the great rampart known as Hadrian's Wall.

In 123 he led a campaign to suppress rebels in Mauretania before moving on through Asia Minor and the islands of the Aegean; in the autumn of 124 he arrived in Greece, for which he had had a fascination from a very young age – he was so fond of learning Greek literature that he was nicknamed *Graeculus*, meaning 'Little Greek'. Hadrian was to spend the winter months touring and reached Athens just in time to preside over the festival of Dionysia in March 125. Then, after visiting Peloponnesus and other parts of Greece, he returned to Rome by way of Sicily in 126. While he was in Sicily coins were struck to celebrate him as being the restorer of the island; unfortunately there is no record today of what he did.

Hadrian's passion for architecture was to inspire him to build some of the most celebrated monuments of the ancient world. The next year was spent in Rome where he saw the completion of the Pantheon, the rebuilding of which had been commissioned by him some years previously. The original Pantheon was built between 27–25BC by the consul Marcus Agrippa as a small temple dedicated to all the Roman gods. Its name is made up from two Greek words, *pan* meaning 'everything' and *theon* meaning 'divine'. Inscribed on the pediment above the portico are the words M·A·GRIPPA·L·F·COS·TERIVM·FECIT meaning 'Marcus Agrippa son of Lucius consul for the 3rd time built this'. The most celebrated feature of the Pantheon is the massive concrete dome; with a span of 142ft (43m) it was, for more than fourteen centuries, the largest dome in the world. In the centre of the dome is the *oculus*, symbolic of the sun; 27ft (8m) in diameter and open to the sky, it is the only source of light. The floor slopes gently to the centre to allow for the runoff of rainwater. According to Roman mythology it stands on the spot where Romulus was carried away to the Gods by an eagle after he had died.

Also completed was Hadrian's villa at nearby Tibur, his retreat near the Sabine Hills. The villa that he built there was on land belonging to his wife and displays some of the finest architecture in the Roman world, featuring many of the places he visited during his life; it was his preferred residence when in Rome and lay only half a day's horse ride from the city. The site spreads over half a square mile and has more than thirty buildings; beneath it lies a network of underground tunnels used by the servants to move goods from one part of the villa to another – some were even wide enough for small wagons. One of the features of the villa is the Canopus, an elongated lake surrounded by a colonnade. This length of water is reminiscent of the canal that gave access to the Canopus at Alexandria.

In the spring of 128 Hadrian set off to visit Africa, but in the summer he returned to Rome from where he set out on his second tour of the empire, a tour that would last for three years. He travelled by way of Athens and Sparta where he dedicated the buildings begun during his first visit. The most important of these was the Olympieum, or the temple of Zeus, for it was well known at the time that Hadrian had assumed the name of Olympius in deference to the gods. In the spring of 129 he visited Asia Minor and Syria and then, having passed the winter at Antioch, went south. The following year Hadrian was to visit Jerusalem, which the Romans had left in ruins after the first Jewish War sixty years before. He at once promised that the ruins would be rebuilt in the name of Aelia Capitolina. On his journey through Egypt he was to restore the tomb of Pompey.

In October 130, while they were travelling through Egypt, his young lover Antinous was drowned in the Nile. The nature of Hadrian's sexuality has been the subject of much speculation and in the hedonistic ways of Rome the love of a man for a boy was considered to be the purest form of love, but love for a woman was deemed as a waste. A woman was an inferior being and only required for procreation; the lust that men felt for them was dirty. Little is known of how Antinous came into Hadrian's life but it is thought that when he was eleven or twelve he was taken from Claudiopolis when Hadrian toured the provinces in 123. Precisely what happened to Antinous is unknown but it is almost certain that his death was by drowning. The *Historia Augusta* (imperial biographies from 117–284) reports the event in the following way:

He lost his Antinous while sailing along the Nile and wept for him like a woman. Concerning this, there are various reports; some assert that he sacrificed himself for Hadrian.

From this point his life was to become one long death wish.

In 133 Hadrian returned to Europe but then a revolt by the Jews forced his return to Palestine. This time it is thought to have broken out because he had founded a colony on the site of Jerusalem and forbidden the ancient Jewish custom of circumcision, an act that both the Romans and Greeks thought of as barbaric. These anti-Jewish acts resulted in a war that was to cost Rome dearly. Troops brought in from Britain and the Danube were to suffer heavy losses; it is thought that an entire legion, *Legio XXII Deiotariana*, was wiped from the face of the earth. Hadrian, leaving the affair in the hands of one of his most trusted generals, returned to Rome in the spring of 134. By this time his health had started to fail and he was to spend the remaining years of his life between the capital and his villa at Tibur.

In 136 Hadrian, having no children of his own, sought an heir before he died. He was now sixty years old and did not want to leave the empire without a leader. Against the advice of all those around him he adopted one Lucius Ceionius Commodus who was to be known as Lucius Aelius Caesar. Though only in his thirties Commodus, too, suffered from ill health and died on 1 January 138. Now under the fear of a challenge to his position as emperor he turned to the wealthy Antoninus Pius, a respected member of the Senate, for adoption; this was on the condition that he, the childless Antoninus, would adopt Hadrian's young nephew Marcus Aurelius and also Lucius Verus, the son of Commodus, as his heirs. In one quick stroke he had ensured the succession for the next two generations.

Hadrian died at his villa at Baiae on 10 July 138 at the age of sixty-two. The cause of his death is believed to have been heart failure: classical sculptures of Hadrian show that he had diagonal earlobe creases, which are synonymous with heart disease. He was first buried at Puteoli on an estate that at one time belonged to Cicero. Later, his remains were moved to Rome where they were buried in the Gardens of Domitia, close by his almost-complete mausoleum.

The mausoleum, once the Mole Adriana and now the Castel Sant' Angelo, is situated on the right bank of the river Tiber near St Peter's. Shaped like a concrete drum, its plan goes back to Etruscan tumuli, via the Mausoleum of Augustus, which lies across the river; the square on which it rests has almost the same dimensions as the Augustus monument. Upon its completion Hadrian's body was cremated and his ashes placed there, together with those of his wife Vibia Sabina and their first adopted son Lucius Aelius, who died in 138. At one time the rooftop was planted with cypresses, or the trees of death, surmounted by a bronze sculpture of Hadrian. In 585 this was replaced by the figure of the Archangel Michael who, when the city was suffering from the plague, was seen to be hovering over the mausoleum. Legend has it that he appeared to be sheathing his sword as a sign that the plague was over.

Throughout his life Hadrian's character was a mass of contradictions; he was as mean as he was generous, cruel as well as being well mannered, eager for fame, yet not vain himself; he was also a homo-sexual. His liking for both good-looking young men as well as women was well known. He was responsible for many changes: the postal service was taken over by the state; people were no longer allowed to hold extravagant banquets; the humane treatment of slaves was strictly enforced; slaves, both male and female, could no longer be sold for immoral and gladiatorial purposes; public baths were kept under strict supervision; and the toga was ordered to be worn in public by Senators.

In spite of his faults, he devoted all of his energy to the state; so much so that his reign could be characterized as a golden age. He was, without doubt, one of the most capable emperors who ever sat on the throne of Rome. For almost twenty-one years he ruled Europe, Northern Africa and the Middle East; it was one of the mightiest empires the world has ever seen. Never again would an emperor live to see so much of his empire: Hadrian had seen it all.

According to the *Historia Augusta*, he composed this poem shortly before his death:

> *Animula, vagula, blandula*
> *Hospes comesque corporis*
> *Quae nunc abibis in loca*
> *Pallidula, rigida, nudula,*
> *Nec, ut soles, dabis iocos…*
> P. Aelius Hadrianus Imp.

> Little soul, gentle and drifting,
> Guest and companion of my body,
> Now you will dwell below in pallid places,
> Stark and bare;
> There you will abandon your play of yore.

CHAPTER II

BUILDING THE WALL

By AD90 Rome had conquered most of Britain and it was only the warlike tribes of Picts, known as the painted people, who prevented advancement in the north. In order to mark the most northerly limits of its empire the Romans were to build walls in both Germany and Britain, set up at the most convenient point across the landscape. In Germany Hadrian had ordered the building of a wooden frontier to mark the edge of the empire; in Britain he felt that a heavily fortified barrier would be better. When he ordered the building of his Wall the Roman army had already been active on the Tyne–Solway isthmus for more than fifty years; this was to be the first frontier line south of Scotland.

It was in 122 that Hadrian landed for the first time on British soil. He had travelled from Germany where he had been inspecting the border defences. The difficulties faced by provincial governors now stared him in the face. For the past two years a rebellion within the province had made it a highly volatile area, and it had become quite apparent that the system of forts and watchtowers along the road later known as the 'Stanegate' was now insufficient to protect its borders. To help him regain control of the frontier zone the concept of building a stone rampart to mark its boundaries then came in to his mind. The wall that he built runs from coast to coast and stretches for 80 Roman miles, from Segedunum at Wallsend in the east to Maia on the shore of the Solway Firth in the west. As with the Great Wall of China it was a means of delineating the border between two ideologies and of controlling movement, and also acted as a trade barrier. The building of the Wall was under the command of Aulus Platorius Nepos and *Legio VI Victrix*. It was to be 10 Roman feet wide (one Roman foot equals 11.7 imperial inches) with a height of 15ft; this was to allow a soldier patrolling the wall to see into the bottom of the ditch, which lay 20ft to the north. A walkway backed the 5ft high battlement. To the south was the military road

Vallum near Carrawburgh.

and Vallum ditch. Eighty small fortlets or 'milecastles' were built, one for every Roman mile; the eightieth was at the western end of the Wall at Bowness-on-Solway. Evenly spaced between the milecastles were pairs of turrets used for observation and signalling.

During the building of the Wall the plan changed several times, and in the west it was reduced and built of turf. This was probably so that the Roman troops could finish the job more quickly; however, most people believe that it was because of lack of stone. The turf Wall did not last very long, and section by section it was all rebuilt in stone. As to the style used in building the milecastles and turrets, much depended on which legion was doing the work, as three different designs have been uncovered.

Construction of the Wall was divided into stretches of about 5 miles (8km); as one group excavated the foundations another would follow on with building the milecastles and turrets. Other cohorts would then follow with the building of the Wall. Shortly after it reached the North Tyne the width of the Wall was reduced to just over 8ft and it became known as the Narrow Wall. However, the Broad Wall foundations had already been laid up to where the turf Wall began; this confirmed that the building of the Wall had been

begun in the east. In total almost four million tons of rocks had to be quarried by hand before the Wall was built. It took almost six years to complete and was then maintained for nearly three hundred years.

Running from coast to coast, the Vallum was an unmistakeable belt of ditch, a prohibited area that lay south of the Wall; its purpose was to enable the Romans to control the movements of anyone who wished to cross from either side. The first reference to the Vallum is made by the early eighth-century historian Bede.

North of the Wall was a V-shaped ditch that made it difficult to cross the Wall at any point other than a milecastle or fort; south of the Wall, the Vallum, with its embankment of earth on each side, could only be crossed at forts or where there were roads. The Vallum ditch was some 20ft wide at the top with a depth of 10ft; on either side of it was flat open ground or berm. Because of the pressure on the ditch from the weight of the wall, the berm was usually 20ft from the ditch. The earth mounds at the edge of the berm were there to slow down any attacking tribe from the south. At Cawfields, the berms of the Vallum are wider on the south than the north.

In a natural gap formed by the valleys of the Tyne and Irthing was the 'Stanegate': the military road built in the days of Agricola, governor of Britannia AD77–85. In the early days it was used to transport the stone required to build the Wall; it also linked the fort at Corbridge with the one at Carlisle that had been built to guard the river crossings on the routes into Scotland. A number of military sites have been uncovered on the road, which suggests that it may have been some form of frontier; forts have been found at Carlisle, Nether Denton, Vindolanda and Corbridge, and fortlets at

The Stanegate road at Corbridge.

The Military Way today.

Haltwhistle Burn and Throp, all of which link to the road. Almost all of the archaeology that relates to the Stanegate sites is pre-Hadrian, yet the road as well as the sites continued to play their part throughout the history of the Wall.

With the withdrawal of Roman troops from Britain in the fourth century, law and order broke down; the abandoned forts soon became little more than shelters for the homeless. The great Wall that Hadrian had built was slowly falling into disrepair, its stones becoming ready-made building material for the locals.

All roads lead to Rome they say, but in the case of Britain this was not the case. Soon after the invasion the Romans realized that this small island had no roads worthy of the name, so they set about building a system that linked their forts. The roads built by them have, over the years, become legendary. They were a vital means of the movement of troops and their supplies, as well as of trade. Some

of those roads are still major routes today and you can drive over long stretches of them. The most striking feature about them is their alignment, for mile after mile they run as straight as an arrow. The base of each Roman road was made of large stones, which was followed by layers of smaller stones, cobbles or gravel and rammed firmly into place; finally the surface would be given a gentle camber. On either side of the road there would be a ditch for drainage. Where it ran through a settlement a stone gutter replaced the ditch, such as can be seen beside the Stanegate at Corbridge.

In 1745 one final act of vandalism took place in the shadow of the Wall. Charged with the interception of Bonnie Prince Charlie in the Rebellion of '45, Wade expected the Pretender to travel south by way of Newcastle and waited for him there; the Prince however used Wade's own roads and headed for Carlisle. Without an adequate road from east to west, he was unable to give relief to the town. After

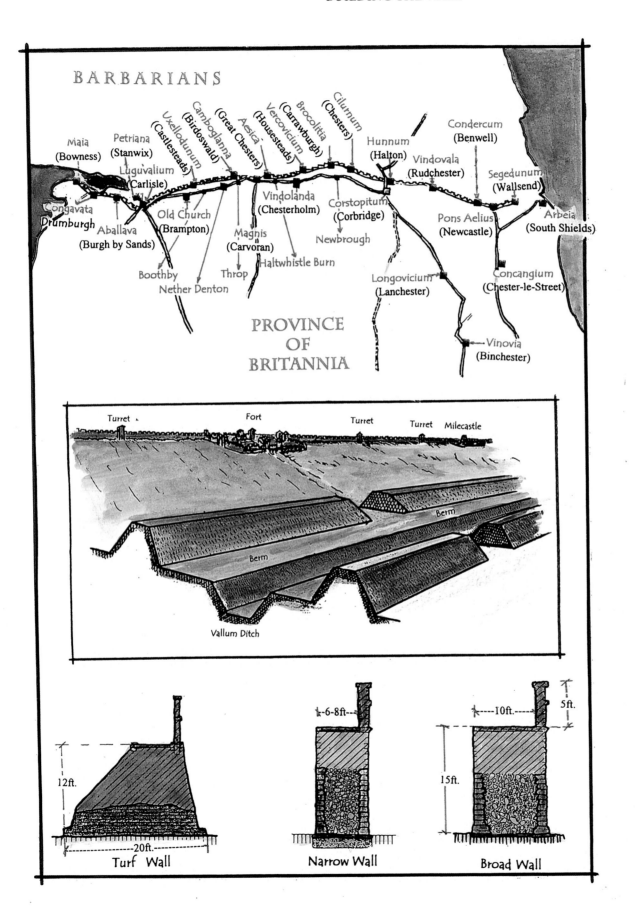

Sketch of Hadrian's Wall route.

the uprising was suppressed a new road known as the Military Road or Wade's Road was built. Now called the B6318 it runs parallel with Hadrian's Wall, and the current state of the wall is partly due to the use of the ready stone in building the road.

Manning the Wall

With the acquisition of overseas provinces the Empire grew and the system of army recruitment came under pressure. Initially all troops were citizens of Rome, but after a series of humiliating defeats in battle there was no option but to re-think the system and allow recruits to come from the provinces. The troops that manned the Wall were auxiliaries, that is non-citizens of Rome; for them Roman citizenship could only be earned by serving twenty-five years with the army. Their numbers, believed to have been in the region of 9,000, fluctuated all through the occupation. The troops garrisoned at the forts were all infantry, all cavalry or a mixture of both; and although the units were at individual forts they were to move about in detachments, making it impossible to determine exact figures. At times they would be withdrawn altogether to serve abroad and may not return for months, if not years. By the fourth century the Empire was in crisis as barbarians threatened even Rome herself; with their garrisons unpaid, most of the forts were abandoned.

The legacy that Rome left behind was not its road building or agricultural methods; it was the binding together of the people. For almost 400 years Rome had brought order and a sense of purpose to Britain that it didn't have before. Before the Romans, the people of Britain had no identity beyond their tribe. In the wake of their departure, every Briton was aware of their identity. No longer were they a nation of warring tribes; they were as one, the people of Britannia.

The Roman Centurion's Song

LEGATE, I had the news last night – my cohort ordered home
By ships to Portus Itius and thence by road to Rome.
I've marched the companies abroad, the arms are stowed below:
Now let another take my sword. Command me not to go!

I've served in Britain forty years, from Vectis to the wall,
I have none other home than this, nor any life at all.
Last night I did not understand, but, now the hour draws near
That calls me to my native land, I feel that land is here.

Here where men say my name was made, here where my work was
    done;
Here where my dearest dead are laid – my wife – my wife and son;
Here where time, custom, grief and toil, age, memory, service love,
Have rooted me in British soil. Ah, how can I remove?

For me this land, that sea, these airs, those folk and fields suffice.
What purple Southern pomp can match our changeful Northern
    skies,
Black with December snows unshed or pearled with August haze –
The clanging arch of steel-grey March, or June's long-lighted days?

You'll follow widening Rhodanus till vine an olive lean
Aslant before the sunny breeze that sweeps Nemausus clean
To Arelate's triple gate; but let me linger on,
Here where our stiff-necked British oaks confront Euroclydon!

You'll take the old Aurelian Road through shore-descending pines
Where blue as any peacock's neck, the Tyrrhene Ocean shines.
You'll go where laurel crowns are won, but – will you e'er forget
The scent of hawthorn in the sun, or bracken in the wet?

Let me work here for Britain's sake – at any task you will –
A marsh to drain, a road to make or native troops to drill.
Some Western camp (I know the Pict) or granite Border keep,
Mid seas of heather derelict, where our old messmates sleep.

Legate, I've come to you in tears – My cohort ordered home!
I've served in Britain forty years. What should I do in Rome?
Here is my heart, my soul, my mind – the only life I know.
I cannot leave it all behind. Command me not to go!

Rudyard Kipling

CHAPTER III

THE STANEGATE FORTS

By AD81 the Roman army, under the leadership of Agricola, had reached far into Scotland, but within the space of three years they had to retreat south to a line between the rivers Tyne and Solway. This line became known as the Trajan frontier. Some 1,200 years later, in medieval times, it was known as the 'Stanegate' or stone road. The Stanegate, which predates the Hadrianic frontier, linked Corbridge and Carlisle, both of which were situated on important routes that linked the south to the north. The first published record of the Stanegate is on John Warburton's map of 1716, where it is shown as an unnamed road branching off from the Military Way. Its route went past the forts at Newbrough and Chesterholm until it reaches Carvoran. The construction of a series of forts along this road allowed many troops to patrol this crucial frontier area. Placed at intervals of 14 Roman miles, which was half a day's march, they were able to quickly bring the area under their governance. By adding a series of smaller watchtowers the forts had much more control. However, the withdrawal from Scotland required the Romans to then provide forts at Newbrough, Carvoran and Brampton Old Church. Of all the Stanegate forts that survive only the remains at Corbridge and Vindolanda hold any interest.

The Stanegate differed from other Roman roads in that it followed the easier gradients whereas typical Roman roads followed a straight path even if this meant having punishing gradients to climb. It began in the east at Corstopitum, at a point where Dere Street (the Roman road from York) heads north to Scotland. West of Corstopitum it crossed the Cor Burn, following the north bank of the Tyne until it reached the North Tyne near the village of Wall. From here it headed west to Newbrough, where the first fort is situated. Continuing west for 6 miles (10km) we then arrive at the fort known as Vindolanda where it crosses the Military Road to pass just south of the minor fort at Haltwhistle Burn. At Haltwhistle Burn the Stanegate then passes the major fort of Magnis before it joins up with the Maiden Way coming up from the south. Here the road turns south-east to follow the River Irthing where it passes the minor fort of Throp; 4½ miles (7km) later it arrives at the major fort

of Nether Denton. From Nether Denton the road continues to follow the River Irthing and heads towards Brampton. Passing the minor fort of Castle Hill Boothby it reaches the major fort of Brampton Old Church. Crossing the River Irthing the road continues east through Irthington and High Crosby. Finally it reaches its terminus, the fort at Luguvalium.

The Stanegate Forts

Corstopitum (Corbridge): major fort.
Newbrough: minor fort.
Vindolanda (Chesterholm): major fort.
Magnis (Carvoran): major fort.
Throp: minor fort.
Nether Denton: major fort.
Castle Hill Boothby: minor fort.
Brampton Old Church: major fort.
Luguvalium (Carlisle): major fort.

Of the Stanegate itself there is now no trace. However, its course is known as it was featured on the first-edition Ordnance Survey map running parallel and to the south of the Wall.

Corbridge

Coria or Corstopitum: Valley of Great Noise
Corbridge is strategically placed on the north bank of the Tyne, where Dere Street crosses the river at its lowest fordable point. The origins of its name are uncertain, but it appears to be from the Latin word *strepitum* meaning 'loud noise'; it also appears on a wooden tablet found at Vindolanda as Coria, which is a Celtic word meaning 'army'. 'Corstopitum', the fort that was built here, predates Hadrian's Wall by some forty-three years; it was built to guard the bridge where

Route of the Stanegate.

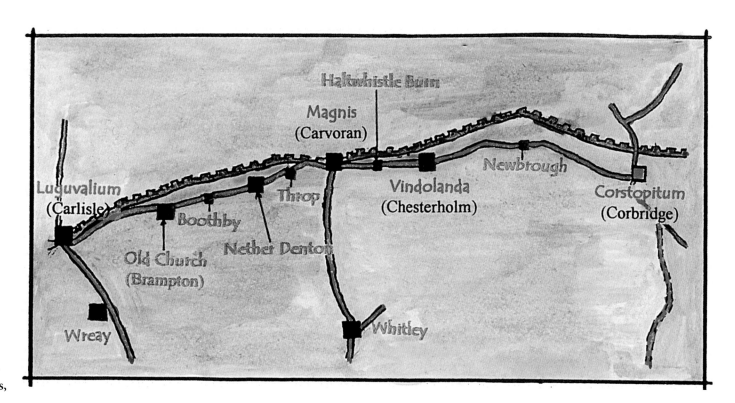

BELOW: Granary portico columns, Corbridge.

Dere Street crossed the Tyne and to act as a supply depot for the Wall. The garrison here was made up of legionary cohorts from the legions that were stationed in Britain. First to arrive was Legio II Augusta from South Wales commanded by Quintus Lollius Urbicus; the last, at the turn of the third century, was *Legio VI Victrix* from York. The hump-backed ground across the southern part of the site is caused by subsidence of earlier forts. What remains of the buildings in this area is only clay and cobble foundations. At the far west of the compound stands the headquarters building with its small strong-room, above which would have been a shrine around which the religious life of the garrison centred.

The garrison that manned the first wooden fort here was likely to have been a cavalry regiment. We can say this with certainty, for in the south transept of Hexham Abbey is a tombstone dedicated to Flavinus, standard-bearer to the *ala Petriana*, showing him riding down his barbarian foe.

The granaries, Corbridge.

The fountain and aqueduct, Corbridge.

The granary air vent, Corbridge.

two pieces from a triangular pediment, which would have crowned this fountain head. These small pieces are large enough to show the original design of the pediment: two winged victories holding between them a circular wreath with the words LEG XX VV FECIT: 'The XX Legion named the *Valeria Victrix* built this.'

According to Roman law a city's cemeteries should stand outside its walls, and in the Wall zone – as elsewhere – it was not unusual for both cremation and inhumations to take place. In 1974, lying to the west of the Cor Burn at Shorden Brae, a Roman mausoleum was found. The purpose for such a large monument in the Roman period was to ensure that a person's name would live on.

Like the fort at South Shields, Corbridge was a major base to the rear of Hadrian's Wall and within its walls are found the best Roman granaries in the country. These buildings, designed to store large quantities of grain, had to have a good circulation of air to keep the grain dry. To achieve this, dwarf stone walls supported the floor and low down, on the outer walls, a series of narrow vents allowed air to circulate in the space under the floor. The loading bays, which faced the Stanegate, were sheltered by porticoes to help protect them from the elements – the columns that supported these porticoes are still to be seen.

At the centre of the town and east of the granaries lay the aqueduct. This brought water down from the north to the fountain house, which was the main distribution point for the public water supply. Though no longer to be seen, an ornamental spout would have directed the flow into the stone trough beyond. The famous Corbridge lion, believed to have been carved as a grave ornament, was later re-used as a fountain head. In the museum on site there are

Surrounding the mausoleum was a precinct wall. Dating from the second century the building measures 32 × 34ft. The square in which it stood was decorated with stone sculptures of lions attacking stags, elements of which were discovered during excavations. Outside the main building stood a much smaller one, which consisted of a central grave and a small outer wall.

The on-site museum at Corbridge, built in the Roman style, displays a rich selection of finds from the site including the famous stone lion.

Chesterholm

Vindolanda: White Meadows
Letter from Octavius to Candidus:

Octavius to his brother Candidus, greetings. The hundred pounds of sinew from Marinus I will settle up. From the time when you wrote about this matter, he has not even mentioned it to me. I have several times written to you that I have bought about five thousand modii of ears of grain, on account of which I need cash. Unless you send me some cash, at least five hundred denarii, the result will be that I shall

Vindolanda Fort.

The fountain, Vindolanda.

lose what I have laid out as a deposit, about three hundred denarii, and I shall become embarrassed. So I ask you send me some cash as soon as possible. The hides which you write about are still at Cataractonium, write that they be given to me and the wagon about which you write. And write to me what is with that wagon. I would have already been to collect them except that I do not care to injure the animals while the roads are bad. See with Terius about the 8½ denarii which he received from Fatalis. He has not credited them to my account. Know that I have completed the 170 hides and I have 119 modii of threshed bracis. Make sure that you send me some cash so that I may have ears of grain on the threshing room floor. Moreover, I have already finished threshing all that I had. A messmate of our friend Frontius has been here. He was wanting me to allocate him some hides, and that being so, was ready to give cash. I told him I would give him some hides by the Kalends of March. He decided that he would come on the Ides of January. He did not turn up, nor did he take the trouble to obtain since he has hides. If he had given the cash, I would have given him them. I hear that Frontinius Julius has for sale at a high price the leather ware which he bought here for five denarii apiece. Greet Spectatus … and Firmus. I have received letters from Gleuco. Farewell.

It had always been assumed that the best accounts of the Roman Empire would come from the arid Middle East; however, among the most important finds ever to be found are the wooden writing tablets that have been found here at Vindolanda. Despite the water-logged conditions in which the tablets were found, many were still legible. So far they have provided us with an insight on the many aspects of daily life that would otherwise have remained unknown. They have surrendered up to us the names of hundreds of individuals, from commanding officers to private soldiers, from officer's wives to personal slaves, from bathhouse orderlies to brewers, pharmacists and clerks. We learn of problems with the weather, of the shortage of beer supplies and of the problems with the roads. We also learn that the 'slang' name for the British is *Brittunculi*, meaning 'wretched little Brits'. The soldiers posted here enjoyed a high standard of living. They ate their meals from ceramic bowls, enjoyed spices from India, fish sauces and Spanish olive oil. Having put 'the meat on the bone' it seems that very little has changed in the 2,000 years since they were written.

Vindolanda, listed in the *Notitia Dignitatum* (*see* Glossary) between the entries for Housesteads and Great Chesters, was one of the supply forts used in the construction of the Wall. It lies in a sheltered valley 2½ miles (4km) to the south-west of Housesteads and guarded the central section of the vital east–west supply route.

Roman milestone, Vindolanda.

Roman Milestone

The approach road to the fort follows the course of the Stanegate; on the north side, and rising to its full height, is the only Roman milestone to be seen standing in Britain where it was originally placed almost 2,000 years ago. A Roman mile was a thousand Roman paces (1,611 yards, 1,473m), so a milestone would be erected every thousand paces. These were round or oval-shaped columns of stone set on a square base; they were between 6–12ft (1.8–3.6m) in height and had a diameter of 30in (76cm). As well as giving distances to the nearest towns, some also had the name of the road builder carved into the stonework. Situated 15 Roman miles west of Corbridge, this milestone is one of the most evocative sights to be seen.

The fort, made of timber, was begun in AD90 as part of the Stanegate garrison; today it is the most remarkable of all the sites in the area. Like most of the forts it has, over the years, been used as a source of building stones, but its remoteness has allowed it to escape the worst of this theft. As far as we know, Vindolanda was never more than a normal garrison fort on the northern frontier, with the wives, children, merchants and slaves living outside the fort walls in the *vicus*. All Roman camps had a *vicus*; part residential for the wives and families of serving men, and for veterans living out their lives on their pensions, and part workshops for the garrison. A *vicus* had the minimum form of self-government that was recognized by Roman law. The settlement grew mainly along the north bank of the Doe Sike to either side of the road coming from the west gate of the fort. Inside the compound, the buildings were taxed according to the length of street they occupied; to avoid high taxes, the shops and dwellings had a narrow frontage.

It is not known who first manned the fort, but we do know that at one time it was garrisoned by the *Cohors I Tungrorum* and the third and ninth Cohorts of Batavians. These were units made up of non-citizen recruits who served for a period of twenty-five years in return for Roman citizenship.

In 1992 the remains of a large building, made up of some fifty rooms, was uncovered, dating from about 120. Both floorplan and the recovered fragments of wall paintings show that this building was something special, for it showed a luxury not previously seen in the province. It is thought that this residence, located midway along the wall, was built for the emperor and his party during his visit in 122.

The museum here houses a unique collection of artefacts found at the site, which tells of what life was like for a Roman soldier.

Roman Temple

The Romans borrowed heavily from the Greeks for their mythology and based their religion on the Greek gods; their belief in magic kept alive the many cults that sprang up around them. The Greek god Zeus became Jupiter; his wife Juno was identified with the Greek goddess Hera. Very popular with the army was Mithras, a god brought from Persia. In Rome the Egyptian goddess Isis had her own temple. One of the most important of all the gods was Vesta, the goddess of the household hearth. Within her circular temple in the Roman Forum was a fire that represented the collective hearth of the state of Rome. This fire was tended by six Vestal Virgins, chosen in childhood, who were bound to the cult for thirty years.

The temple, Vindolanda.

Altar dedicated to Syria, Carvoran.

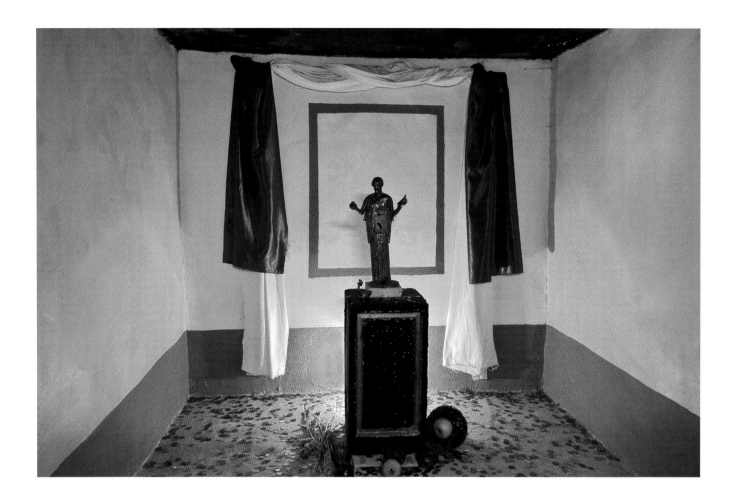

Carvoran

Magnis: Place of Stone

The fort at Carvoran lies at the junction of the Stanegate and the Maiden Way, the road that ran south through the Pennines. In the days of Hadrian, the garrison was manned by the First Cohort of Hamian archers, who came from Syria. Their commander, Flavius Secundus, had an alter set up to the adopted son of Hadrian, Lucius Aelius Caesar.

The purpose of Carvoran was to guard the road junction and the important gap of the Tipalt valley. In the *Notitia Dignitatum* it appears as Magnis, between the entries for Aesica and Camboglanna. In 1599, Camden saw it 'within two furlongs of Caervoran, on a pretty high hill the Wall is still standing, fifteen feet in height, and nine in breadth'. This must have been on the edge of the crags of the Nine Nicks of Thirlwall.

Aerial photography of the site has revealed a large enclosure to the south-west, and the northward diversion of the Vallum here suggests the presence of an earlier large fort, known as Magna. In 1915, just to the north of the fort, was what appeared to be an old bucket sticking out of the ground. However this turned out to be a Roman *modius*, or dry measure in bronze. Conical in shape, it stands about a foot high and was made towards the end of the first century, during the reign of the Emperor Domititian. It weighs almost 26lb and nominally held 17½ *sextarii*, or 16.8 pints. Its actual capacity is, however, 20 pints and it has been suggested that the difference was a means used to defraud farmers when they delivered their wheat; but Roman measures are normally quite accurate and this assumption seems unlikely.

Since the early medieval period Carvoran has been robbed of its stone, the lords of Blenkinsopp being among the culprits – they used the material from the site to construct their castle. The Vindolanda Trust now owns Carvoran and the Roman Army Museum, both of which are an excellent introduction to life on the Wall. There is also an excellent video to be seen that shows Hadrian's wall though the eyes of an eagle.

Brampton Old Church

About a mile from the centre of Brampton, built on the site of a Stanegate fort and using its stone, is the parish church of Brampton. The fort at Brampton Old Church was founded during the early Trajanic period at a time when the Stanegate frontier was being strengthened. Its clay rampart was built on a foundation of river cobbles between stone kerbs, and its internal buildings were of stone. Like the stone fort at Castlesteads it was about 400sq ft in size. The *praetentura*, the front part of the fort, lies together with the *via principalis* beneath St Martins church and its large graveyard. Due to the lack of evidence, it is thought that the fort was only occupied up to the point when the garrisons moved from the Stanegate to the line of the Wall.

St Martin's Churchyard, Brampton Old Church.

Carlisle

Luguvalium: Luguvalos Town

As well as being the home of the Carvetii tribe, Luguvalium was an important centre. Better known as Carlisle, it was the largest town in the wall area and most north-westerly town in the Roman Empire. The fort that was built here guarded the western end of the Stanegate; it was rebuilt several times, first in wood and later in stone. It acted as a supply depot and headquarters for the western part of Hadrian's Wall. However, with the building of the Wall, the front-line troops moved to the new and larger fort north of the river Eden at Stanwix. The first clear evidence of a fort on the site came to light when the foundations were being laid for an extension to Tullie House in 1892, when parts of a turf and timber structure were found, sited to guard the Eden. Tullie House, a converted Jacobean mansion, has been a museum and art gallery since the early part of the nineteenth century and within its grounds are the only visible remains of the town that was known as Luguvalium. Visitors to the museum are able to travel back in time and discover what this frontier region was really like.

In 2001 archaeologists unearthed what was to be the most significant find of Roman artefacts in fifty years. Weapons, siege equipment and some of the best-preserved armour ever to be discovered were found at the waterlogged site. Also found were leather bindings and complex iron scales joined by bronze wire; these were thought to protect cavalrymen's shoulders. The finds were discovered during a dig on the site of Carlisle's new Millennium Gallery by the site of the Roman fort.

Gravestone of lady, Tullie house.

CHAPTER IV

EAST OF THE STANEGATE: WALLSEND TO CORBRIDGE

Edge of the Empire

The empire Rome built over 1,000 years would never be as big or as confident again as it was during Hadrian's reign. Five years after coming to the throne he decided to visit some of his far-flung provinces. His first visit was to the Rhine frontier. Known as the *limes*, this was a wooden palisade that stretched from the North Sea to the Rhine.

By the time Hadrian arrived in Britain at the end of 121 the province was beginning to settle down to the Roman way of life. Prior to his arrival there had been a major rebellion for almost two years and he had come to see for himself what was causing the constant bellicosity of the tribes; this was to be no peacetime tour. With the newly appointed governor Aulus Platorius Nepos by his side, Hadrian decided on a course of action. Until now no other emperor had spent time in Britain, so Hadrian took this opportunity to make his mark. The barrier that he built in northern Britain made the edge of Roman power very visible. Unlike the German *limes*, which was built in wood, this barrier would be made of stone. Built by three of the four legions stationed in Britain – the II, VI and XX – the Wall and its earthworks looked both ways. It announced to everyone that the Romans were in control of all movement and that they could seal off any place at any time. The Wall would separate the civilized world from the barbarians.

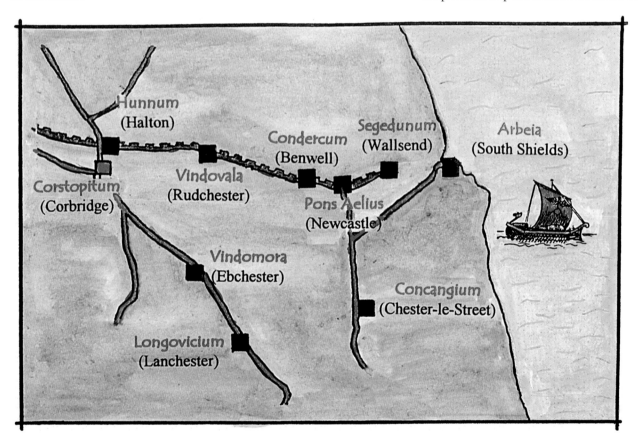

Route east of the Stanegate.

Arbeia west gate.

South Shields

Arbeia: the place of the Arabs
The River Tyne looked different 2,000 years ago: its entrance, though wide, had banks that were lined with mud flats and beds of reed. When Hadrian visited in 122 the Romans had already been there forty years. Being on the other side of the river, Arbeia was not strictly a wall fort, but it was an important post. South Shields was called Tunnocelum in Roman times and the Tyne, on which it stood, was a very important river; for at its mouth was the starting point of one of the army's great marching routes, the Tenth *Iter* of Antonine. The strongly fortified fort that was built here was known as Arbeia; its name, taken from the Aramaic, means 'Place of the Arabs'. Originally built during the reign of Hadrian, it is the most easterly of the garrisoned forts and, sitting on the south bank of the Tyne, had become well known as a great trade centre as well as a fort.

The first two units stationed here were 'wings' of a cavalry unit, each having in the region of 500 men. One of them was the *Ala I Pannoniorum Sabiniana*, recruited from the Pannonian tribes of modern day Hungary; the other, from north-west Spain, was the *Ala I Hispanorum Asturum*. These units were part of the army that had accompanied Claudius in his invasion of AD43. In 208 a 1,000-strong infantry unit, the *Cohors V Gallorum*, replaced the two cavalry units, and the fort then became a supply base to the legions. The *V Gallorum* left many of the artefacts that have been found here.

Tombstones have been found to be the most common of all remains left by the Romans. One of the most spectacular finds at Arbeia is the one dedicated to Regina, wife and former slave of Barates. It is unique in having its inscription in two languages. The first part of the inscription is in Latin and reads 'To the spirits of the dead. Regina, a freedwoman and wife of Barates of Palmyra, a Catuvellauni by race, thirty years old.' The tribe of the Catuvellauni was the largest in Britain and centred themselves on what is now St Albans. Barates, her husband, came from the desert city of Palmyra in Syria. His first language would have been Aramaic, which accounts for the change made in the final line 'Regina, freedwoman of Barates, alas!' Barates' own epitaph was found at Corbridge, where he had died at the age of sixty-eight. His tombstone tells us that he had been

Arbeia commandant's house.

**Model of
Wallsend Fort.**

a travelling merchant who supplied military standards to the Roman army. Regina's tombstone tells us of the unlikely meeting between two people of the Roman Empire who came from provinces that were furthest apart, Britannia and Syria. She is seen seated on a high-backed wicker chair in the pose and dress of the Roman matron, wearing a necklace of large beads. In her hand she carries her spindle and distaff as evidence of her position. At her feet are other symbols of her role as diligent manager, a strong box and a basket of wool.

Standing at the south-east corner, not at the centre as is normal, is the reconstructed courtyard house of the commanding officer. The building is Roman in style and has several rooms laid out around the courtyard, one of which is the *triclinium*, or dining room. Some of the frescos seen in the rooms have been copied from fragments of plaster found on site.

In 1866, when the nave of Jarrow church was being rebuilt, two inscribed Roman stones were found. Ian A. Richmond and R.P. Wright translated the one that was donated to the Society of Antiquities. It reads 'The emperor Caesar Traianus Hadrianus Augustus son of all his divine ancestors, decided it was necessary on

the advice of the gods to fix the boundaries of the Empire in the second consulship…'.

Wallsend

Segedunum: the strong fort
From the Pons Aelius (*see* below) the Wall had reached Chesters in the west before a change in plan was made to extend it east to Wallsend. The first visible signs of the Wall are in the stretch attached to the south-east corner of the fort at Segedunum, where it joined the 4-acre fort to the river. Built by Legio II Augusta to hold the eastern end of the Wall, the port was built within the precincts of the Wall.

Little remains of this fort that at one time would have held close to 600 men. Like all other Roman encampments it is in the shape of a playing card. The headquarters – the principia – was positioned at the fort's centre; it was from here that the troops were paid and justice dispensed. Next to it stood the commanding officers' house, or *praetorium*. The fort also had ten barrack blocks, a granary, a hospital and a bath house. It has often been asked 'where did they put the horses in Roman forts?' Excavations carried out by archaeologists at Segedunum have answered the question. Each barrack block was for a single troop of cavalry; the horses would live in the front rooms and the men at the rear.

Although the site of the original bath house is not known for certain, it is believed to have been to the south of the fort; lying within the *vicus*. The reconstructed bath house is a mirror image of the one at Chesters fort and gives a much better idea of how a bath house would have looked. In Hadrian's day there were a number of large bath houses in Rome that held several hundred bathers at a time; each town or city would have its own baths and every fort on the Wall was equipped with one.

Today a panoramic view of the site can be obtained by climbing to the top of the superb viewing tower; over 100ft (30m) in height, it stands over the museum and visitor centre. Open to the public all the year round, it is a 'must see' for anyone interested in Roman Britain. At one time, it is believed that a monument of Hadrian stood at the end of the Wall at this point.

The hot room at Wallsend bath house.

Swing bridge, site of Pons Aelius, Newcastle.

Pons Aelius

Bridge of Hadrian

The Emperor Hadrian was first to realize the importance of the river when he bridged the steep-sided valley of the Tyne; known as Pons Aelius, this new bridge carried the road from the existing fort at Concangis (Chester-le-Street). During their almost 400 years of occupation the Romans built three bridges over the Tyne: one on the site of the present swing-bridge, the second at Corbridge and the third at Chesters. In 1872 the site of the Aelian Bridge was found lying beneath that of the swing-bridge. The bridge had two stone abutments, and of the ten piers thought to have supported it, only two have been located. Its length from bank to bank is thought to have been in the region of 735ft (220m). In 1875 and 1903 two altars were dredged from the river; dedicated respectively to Neptune and Oceanus, they came from a bridge shrine intended to protect it from tides and floods.

33

The keep at Newcastle.

Newcastle

Newcastle was originally the point where the Wall started. The fort that stood here, although quite small, was sited to guard an important river crossing and mark the Wall's terminus; however, it was not long before an extension eastward to the fort at Segedunum pushed it into second place. The *Notitia Dignitatum* records that in the early fourth century the fort was garrisoned by the First Cohort of Cornvii from Wroxeter; recruited from the tribe itself, they are the only native British unit known to have served in Britannia. The Cornvii were a Celtic race who lived in the present day counties of Cheshire, Shropshire and north Staffordshire. The first mention of the tribe occurs in the works of Ptolemy in the second century.

A short time ago the remains of the fort were found, together with what was left of the *praetorium* and *principia* beside the castle keep; the remainder of the fort lies buried beneath the castle. Today, like the Romans, we can still reach the riverside via the steep stairs that descend from the postern gate of the castle. The Wall itself runs just north of the Roman Catholic Cathedral in the centre of the city.

Museum of Antiquities

On the edge of the Haymarket, in the unlikely setting of Newcastle University, is housed the greatest collection of Roman finds in the north. Among its most notable items are the Aesica brooch and the Aemilia finger-ring; also to be seen is the Bear Cameo from South Shields. In addition to a scale model of Hadrian's Wall there is also a full-scale reproduction of a *Mithraeum*, a temple to Mithras. Masterpieces in Roman art include the Birth of Mithras stone from Housesteads; this depicts the earliest signs of the zodiac found in Britain. The museum is a treasure house of discoveries.

Benwell

Condercum: a place with good views
Nothing remains of the Wall from Wallsend until Benwell is reached, where the fort sat astride the Wall. It is known from several building inscriptions that the *Legio II Augusta* built the first defences of the fort at Benwell. It was built to oversee the Denton Burn stream, which lies to the west and flows into the Tyne. Its size would suggest that it was to be manned by a part-mounted unit. Indeed, in the second century the fort is known to have been garrisoned by *Cohors I Vangionum Milliaria Equitata*; a part-mounted unit from Germany with a nominal strength of 1,000 men. At the foot of a suburban crescent in Denhill Park are the remains of a crossing point over the Vallum leading to the fort's south gate. Discovered in 1935 by Professor Eric Birley, it is the only Vallum gateway to be seen today along the line of the Wall. Spanning the Vallum was an arched gateway that was closed by double doors to stop wheeled traffic coming up from the south. These crossings were sited every 45yd (40m) or so, constructed by putting the material from the breach made in the mounds back into the ditch.

In what appears to be someone's front garden stands the foundations of a tiny temple to a long-forgotten god; a reminder of the settlement that once was. Dedicated to a god named Antenociticus, the temple lies about 100 yards outside the precincts of the fort. This god is not mentioned on any known Roman altar stones and is therefore thought to be a British deity; he has only been found at Benwell. The building, small and rectangular in shape, measures 10 × 16ft (3 × 5m); an asp, where a life-sized image of the god was placed, extends it a further 6ft (1.8m).

When the temple was excavated in 1862, as well as the arms and legs from his statue, three altar stone were found. One inscription tells us 'For the god Antenociticus. By the decrees of the best and greatest of our emperors, under [the administration of] the consular

ABOVE: **Venus with nymphs, Museum of Antiquaries.**

BELOW: **The temple of Antenociticus at Benwell.**

Ulpius Marcellus, while serving as a prefect of cavalry, Tineius Longus was adorned with the broad stripe [of a senator] and appointed to the post of Quaestor'.

The 'best and greatest of emperors' was Commodus, who fought as a gladiator before the plebeians in Rome. Ulpius Marcellus was Governor of Britain in 180.

ABOVE: The Vallum crossing at Benwell.

Denton turret and wall.

Stretch of wall at Heddon-on-the-Wall.

Denton Turret

Apart from the short stretch of Wall seen at Wallsend, the first length of Wall that we see *in situ* is at Denton Burn. Along the West Road, just before the slip road to the A1M, stands a short stretch of Wall and the remains of a turret. The Wall here is entirely of 'Broad' Wall dimensions, unlike Wallsend, and was built to its full width and height before it was changed to 'Narrow' Wall dimensions. As well as the stretch of wall, there are also the remains of a turret; turrets were two-storey structures, built of stone and measuring 14ft (4.2m) square. The ground floor often contained fireplaces and was used as a mess by off-duty soldiers; a timber ladder led from the ground floor up to the lookout post on the upper floor.

Heddon-on-the-Wall

At Heddon-on-the-Wall, some 7 miles (11km) west of Newcastle, we see the first visible section of the wall. It was here, in 1752, that a large hoard of Roman coins in wooden boxes was found in almost mint condition. The stretch of Broad Wall here is impressive and is the longest section of Broad Wall standing today – west of here the Romans built the Narrow Wall on the foundations of the Broad Wall. From Heddon the Military Road runs east in an almost straight line. The village itself stands on the site of a milecastle where a hoard of Roman coins was found in 1879.

Rudchester Fort

Vindobala: White Point

The name for the Roman fort that stood at Rudchester is recorded in the *Notitia Dignitatum* as Vindobala; it falls between the entries for the forts at Benwell and Halton Chesters. It covered an area of about 4 acres and, like all Roman forts, it was in the shape of a playing card. Built across the Wall, it was garrisoned by a mixed cohort of infantry and cavalry.

It is a site rich in shrines. Excavations have found a life-size statue of Hercules as well as five altars belonging to the temple of Mithras and the sun god Apollo. Also revealed are signs of the fort's tumultuous past: towards the end of the second century it was burned to the ground; it was later rebuilt only to be abandoned a century later. The death knell of the fort was when it was ransacked for stone to build the Military Road. The last reference to it was made in the eighteenth century by the archaeologist Alexander Gordon who remarked:

> The ruins within the fort plainly appear, and the entries into it may be distinguished. If there has been a town without, which there can be any doubt of; it has been as usual on the south where the village of Rutchester now stands, and covers its ruins.

Nothing remains of the site today.

Altar stone found at Halton Chesters.

Halton Chesters

Hunnum: The Rock

Urban sprawl has seen off most of the Wall between Newcastle and Corbridge, and only the walker will see more than the Vallum. Halfway between milecastles 21 and 22 stood the fort at Halton Chesters; as at Rudchester, nothing remains and it holds little of interest for today's traveller. The site, standing on a small plateau and marked only by a small clump of trees and a pair of stone gate posts, is very easy to pass by. Built by the *Legio VI Victrix* the fort, almost square in shape, lay across the Wall and had a garrison of infantry with cavalry support. It lies about 2½ miles (1.5km) from Corstopitum. Within the *vicus* found on the southern side of the Wall are the remains of a temple. About half a mile (800m) west of the fort, crossing the Wall at Port Gate, lies Dere Street, the north–south road from Corbridge. The remains of the gate still stood here as recently as 1732.

When Hutton passed this way in 1801 he had this to say: 'I passed through the centre of this station without knowing it, till an intelligent gentleman set me right.'

Altar stone found at Rudchester.

CHAPTER V

NORTH OF THE STANEGATE: CORBRIDGE TO CARLISLE

AD43, like 1066, is one of those dates that stands out in British history. For it was the year that Claudius, Emperor of Rome, sent four of his legions to conquer this small island. Claudius was the uncle of the megalomaniac Caligula who, two years earlier, had been assassinated by his own Praetorian Guard. In the summer of AD40 Caligula had made an abortive attempt to invade Britain. After briefly putting to sea he ordered his legionaries to gather seashells from the beach, claiming that he had won a great triumph over Neptune: the shells were then taken back to Rome to be displayed as 'spoils of war'.

In AD54 Claudius died, thought to have been poisoned by his stepson Nero. AD60 saw the revolt of Boudicca, queen of the tribe of the Iceni in what is now Norfolk. This came about following the death of her husband Prasutagus, who had made his two daughters, as well as the emperor, heir to his kingdom. Nero, refusing to share power with the daughters of Prasutagus, gave orders to take the kingdom by force. Publicly flogged, and with her daughters raped, Boudicca fought back. She scorned the Romans living under Nero by saying that they were 'slaves to a lyre-player' and comparing Roman

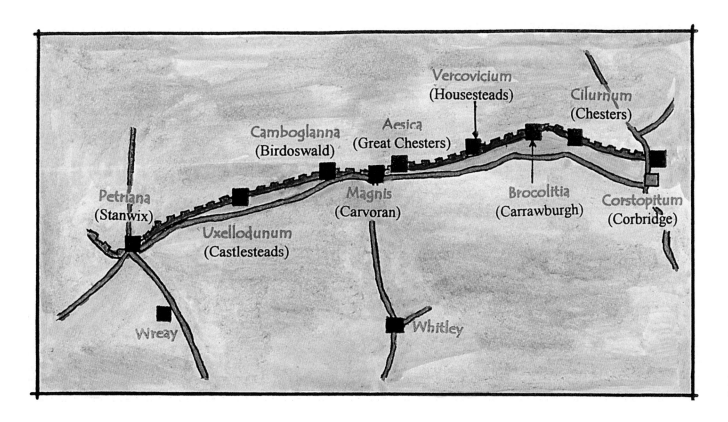

Route north of the Stanegate.

rule to 'hares trying to rule wolves'. Raising a vast army she led them south into the heart of the colonists, where almost 80,000 died in the bloodbath that followed. The Roman historian Tacitus wrote:

They could not wait to cut throats, hang, burn or crucify their victims. In the groves of their terrible dark goddess Andraste, they tortured their captives to death, sewing the severed breasts of the women to their lips and impaling others on stakes driven through their bodies. No cruelty was too great. When the oppressed rise up against cruel oppressors, restraint is rare.

First to face Boudicca was *Legio IX Hispania*; despite their fierce reputation they were routed. As she moved into the flat lands of the midlands she met Suetonius Paulinus, Governor of Britain, head-on. Finally, after unleashing all of her fury on his legions, Boudicca lost the battle. As she lay dying, she is said to have put a curse on the legions that had destroyed her people; a curse that would be recalled some sixty years later. On a bleak morning one day in 117, it was said, the 5,000 men of the Ninth Legion marched north to fight the barbarians; they were never heard of again.

The legend of the 'lost' Ninth Legion draws on stories that embroider the fact that it appears to have disappeared around 117. A list of all active legions made in the reign of Marcus Aurelius (161–180) does not include it, implying that it had ceased to exist. The conjecture that it was wiped out by the Caledonians and brought about the building of Hadrian's Wall has been attractive to many authors, most famously Rosemary Sutclif, author of the bestselling *The Eagle of the Ninth*. However, Roman legions were occasionally annihilated and their numbers cancelled, most famously the three legions that were destroyed by Arminius in the Teutoberg forest in AD9. But the more prosaic truth of *IX Hispania* is that inscriptions show that the legion was moved to a base in Holland; it is thought that it may have been lost in action whilst dealing with the Judean revolt in AD132.

Planetrees

At either side of the fort at Chesters there are a number of sections of Wall that can be clearly seen from the road. As the Wall makes its

The wall at Planetrees.

Brunton turret.

long descent down the slope from Planetrees towards Brunton turret, we can see the Wall beginning to change from Broad Wall to Narrow Wall.

When William Hutton passed this way in 1801 it was in the process of being dismantled to build a farmhouse. The sight of workmen carrying out this wilful destruction caused him to burst into tears; they had already demolished 224yd (204m) before he had arrived. Hutton tells us that the farmer's name was Henry Tulip, and what stands today is down to the entreaties that Hutton made to him.

Brunton Turret

At Brunton turret, with almost a third of the Wall complete, a significant change took place. Up to this point the Wall had been built to a 10ft (3m) gauge known as the Broad Wall, but hereafter a much narrower specification was used. The reason for this is unclear, although it was probably to speed things up. The tower, known as turret 26b, is a good place to see this change because you can see both the 10ft foundations and the narrow curtain wall subsequently built there. It tells us quite a lot about how the Wall was constructed: the turrets and milecastles were built first, then the curtain wall.

From Brunton turret the Wall ran in a straight line to the North Tyne and the bridge leading to the fort at Chesters.

Chesters Bridge Abutment

Surprisingly little is known about bridges in Roman Britain: they were usually made of timber, so naturally none have survived. Before reaching its terminus at Bowness the Wall had three major rivers to cross: the North Tyne east of Chesters, the River Irthing west of Willowford and the Eden, between Carlisle and Stanwix. Of these crossings only the remains of the first two survive.

The river at Chesters was the first major obstacle on the route from east to west. To enable the Wall to continue and cross the river, a timber bridge was built at this point. The first bridge, built under Hadrian, had eight stone piers but the second, built in the third century, had only three; even so, it was wide enough for a chariot to cross. One pier of the bridge is buried in the riverbank, while two others and the west abutment have been detected in the river itself. At times, when the river is low, the bridge abutment of the western side and two piers can be seen lying beneath the water. A feature to look out for is the phallus symbol carved for luck on the northward outer face of the abutment.

To the west of the abutment, rows of geometric stones lie exposed to the elements. Excavated from the river by Clayton in the nineteenth century, it is not known what part of the bridge they came from. The pioneering archaeologist William Stukeley suggests that extra-large blocks 'having intervals between, sufficiently large for the passage of the water', were used in the foundations of the river bridge.

Chesters Fort

Cilurnum: the cauldron pool

This large fort covers an area of 5¾ acres (2ha) and has the classic 'playing card' layout; it is the best-preserved example of a Roman cavalry fort in Britain. The name of Chesters is first mentioned in the late fourth century where it is listed as Cilurnum in the *Notitia Dignitatum*. It was built to house cavalry that was capable of rapid strikes into the 'barbaric' north. As is usual for all cavalry forts on the Wall, it was built on the line of the barrier, with three of its gateways opening to the north side. A road issuing from the south gateway linked it to the old Stanegate. Aerial photography has revealed that a small *vicus* existed on either side of this road.

Foundation stones at Chesters.

Chesters fort museum.

LEFT: Bridge abutment (east side of river) at Chesters.

The barracks, Chesters.

There is a lot to see here; all four of the principal gateways are well preserved. The foundations of the fort are clearly laid out, and the headquarters building, the regimental temple and strong room can be quite clearly seen.

An integral part of the Roman fort is its barracks. At Cilurnum they were sited in the north-east area of the fort, north of the *principia*. The Asturian cavalry who formed the garrison here came from the mountainous area of northern Spain; an area that can be as cold as the North Tyne valley. The entrance to the barracks was covered by a veranda walkway supported by columns, some of whose bases remain. A deep stone drainage gutter runs through the middle of the street between the barrack blocks. When these blocks were excavated they were found to be full of pottery, bones, oyster shells and all kinds of rubbish that gave an insight on the eating habits of the soldiers. None of the buildings we can see today is exposed in its full length.

One of the most luxurious buildings in the fort is the commandant's house. This was because the commander of a cavalry unit was often a man of considerable rank and political standing. The dwelling rooms and baths were heated by means of a 'hypocaust': the smoke and hot air from a furnace were drawn under the floors of the rooms, which were supported on pillars of burnt clay tiles; brick tiles

Commandant's
hypocaust,
Chesters Fort.

The bath house
at Chesters.

were used because the heat would have cracked stone. So as to prevent the smoke coming up through the floors, the floors of the rooms were double slabs of stones cemented together. The stone pillars that can be seen in the photograph are an irregularity due to a partial reconstruction in the fourth century.

The bath house at Cilurnum, situated close to the river outside the fort walls, is one of the best preserved on the line of the Wall. It was built outside the fort walls close to where the bridge crossed the river. From the high ground a flight of wooden steps lead down to the original entrance. Here, an outer lobby leads into what appears to be the disrobing and anointing chamber, with seven round-arched niches on the west wall. Though nothing certain is known about their use, it is believed that they may have been cupboards for the bathers to hang their clothes in. From here one passes into a lobby, which gives access to the hot room on the right and the cold rooms on the left. Through another lobby, which lies directly ahead, is the final 'rest and amusement room', which has flues in the form of a cross. To the right of this room lies another chamber, also with cross flues, with a semi-circular apse out of which opens a splayed window. Outside, beneath this window, fragments of glass of a bluish green colour have been found. In Roman times glass was not as transparent as it is now. For windows it was made by pouring molten glass onto a flat surface. Two hot rooms, one leading through to the other, are heated by hypocausts.

In the first century the poet Seneca, who lived for a time above a bath house, gave a colourful account of the lively world of the baths:

I would die if silence were as necessary to study as they say. I live just above a bath house. Consider all the hateful voices I hear! When the fat men do their exercise with lead weights, I hear their groans and gasps. Or when someone else comes in to get a vulgar massage: I hear the slap of the masseur's hand on his flesh. The commotion caused by a thief caught stealing. Add those who leap into the pool with a huge splash. Besides these, who at least have normal voices, consider the hair plucker, always screeching for customers, and never quiet except when he's making someone else cry. The incessant cries of the cake-seller and sausage seller, each with his peculiar tone and style. (Seneca: letter 56)

The *sacellum* at Chesters.

ABOVE: **Black Carts turret.**

BELOW: **Ditch and wall at Black Carts.**

The *aerarium* was the secure storage area for the army pay chest. It was located underground and for security was cut into the natural bedrock. It was here that the deferred pay of the soldiers was deposited until it was due, or until their discharge; it was also where the army kept their pay-sheets. In the early part of the nineteenth century the oak strong room door, studded with nails, was uncovered – unfortunately, once it had been exposed to air it fell apart. The legions' standards were stored in the room above known as the *sacellum*.

A vast collection of Roman finds discovered by John Clayton, who at one time owned this site, can be found in the museum.

Black Carts Turret

Two miles (3km) west of Chesters, lying parallel to the road, is the Black Carts turret. The turret, first unearthed in 1873, measures 11ft 10in × 11ft 4in (3.6 × 3.45m). The back wall of the turret is eleven courses high, but at the front it is almost gone. The adjacent wall is built to the narrow width, so this is the first turret that we see having wing-walls of the broad gauge on both sides. As we travel west this long stretch of Wall is broken by the branch road that leads to Simonburn.

Heading towards Limestone Corner, the land starts to rise. To the right Chipchase Castle and the wild Northumbria countryside; to the left the ditch and Wall. The ditch, although overgrown, is full of interest. By analysing the soil samples taken from here, archaeologists have now learned that the south mound of the Vallum was built first.

Limestone Corner

At Limestone Corner the Wall once again coincides with the road, though much of it survives as a buried feature. The ditch is deep, the Vallum and both mounds plain to see. It is here one has an idea of just how difficult it could be for the soldiers; at this point they had to cut through solid rock and dislodge large stones without the aid of

Rocks for cutting, Limestone Corner.

The ditch at Limestone Corner.

Temple of Mithras at Brocolitia.

power tools or explosives. It is worth noting that, while the Wall ditch is unfinished, the Vallum on the summit has been fully dug. Looking west we can see what they had to contend with.

The Romans would split the rocks by chiselling holes in them and then inserting wooden wedges that had been soaked in water. Over time these would swell and split the rock along its natural line. In the ditch, on the summit of Limestone Corner, the large stone blocks lie where they were abandoned almost 2,000 years ago.

Carrawburgh: Temple of Mithras

Brocolitia: the badger holes

> Mithras, God of the midnight, here where the great bull dies,
> Look on Thy children in darkness. Oh take our sacrifice!
> Many roads Thou has fashioned: all of them lead to the Light!
> Mithras, also a soldier, teach us to die aright!
> Rudyard Kipling: 'A Song to Mithras'

Brocolitia, listed between the entries for Chesters and Housesteads in the *Notitia Dignitatum*, lies just over a mile (1.6km) from mile-

castle 30. Visitors to the site can see the temple dedicated to Mithras in its fourth-century phase, which was first unearthed in 1949 when a colleague of John Gillam told him he had 'found something interesting at Carrawburgh'. Three days later he was at the site with friends when they found the temple of Mithras; they were the first people to see the three altars since the forth century.

Of all the mysteries left to us by antiquity, few are more intriguing than the worship of Mithras: a religion that was centred on the so-called tauroctony, or bull-slaying scene. This was a secret only revealed to those who were accepted into the cult. The *mithraea*, as the temples were known, were often built underground so that they emulated the cave in which Mithras had killed the bull; oil lamps were used to heighten their sense of mysticism.

Although the cult of Mithras has its origins in India, the Roman Army first encountered it in Persia, during the reign of Nero. Exclusive to men, it emphasized honour and was divided into seven grades, each one marking a point of knowledge in the cult's mysteries. Each supplicant wore a costume and headmask to symbolize his grade, and had to undergo severe tests: he began at the first stage as a *Corax* (raven), then progressed through all the stages until reaching the ultimate stage of *Pater* (father). For five hundred years it was the religion of the Roman Army.

Coesike Turret (33b)

Two and a half miles (4km) beyond Carrawburgh the road swings left and crosses the Vallum. Turret 33b stands about 150 yards (140m) east of the twenty-seventh milestone at the bridge crossing the Coesike. The turret is of the type built by the Twentieth Legion, though an inscription by the Sixth Legion was found in the blocking of the doorway. When it fell out of use its square interior, originally let into the Wall, was reduced and the Wall brought up to full width. At the end of the second century it was abandoned altogether.

Milecastle 35 at Sewingshields.

Sewingshields Milecastle

At Sewingshields the Wall at last climbs to the crest of the Whin Sill. Here, at 1,068ft (325m) above sea level, the Crags fall dramatically away beneath your feet. From milecastle 35 the Wall winds its way along the crest up to the fort at Housesteads. Best known for its views, Sewingshields Crags also has links with King Arthur. Somewhere beneath the crag, between King's Crag and Queen's Crag, stands a large boulder and cave associated with this legendary king. In the cave, King Arthur, Queen Guinevere and the Knights of the Round Table are said to lie sleeping until the people of England call on them in their hour of need. On a table nearby sits a horn, a sheathed sword and a garter. To awaken the sleeping group one must

draw the sword, cut the garter and blew the horn. Years ago a farmer found his way into this cave where, knowing the legend, he drew the sword and cut the garter, but forgot to blow the horn. Arthur woke for a brief second from his sleep to exclaim:

O woe betide that evil day,
On which this witless wight was born,
Who drew the sword, the garter cut,
But never blew the bugle-horn

From the summit one can see the earthworks of Black Dyke running towards the Wall from the north.

The Wall near to King's Wicket.

The Great Whin Sill

The Great Whin Sill, one of the most outstanding geographical features in England, took its name from terms used by quarrymen: 'whin' was a hard dark rock and a 'sill' was a flat-lying layer of rock. Formed by volcanic and seismic activity rather than glacial movement, it stretches in an 80-mile (130km) arc from Kirby Stephen in Cumbria to the North Sea at Bamburgh. From milecastle 35, on the slopes of Sewingshields Crags, we begin to traverse the most spectacular stretch of Wall; before us a rollercoaster of sheer cliffs show the full drama of the Whin Sill. It is here that the Roman frontier begins its long march along its crest. Descending from the trig point, we look northward to the rough, open country of the barbarian. Both Busy Gap and King's Wicket were well known access points to the Border Reivers (cross-border raiders).

Knags Burn Gate

At Knags Burn, we see one of the few gates through the Wall that was not at a fort or milecastle. Overlooked by the fort at Housesteads, it was for the use of civilians. Pivot-holes show that at one time the gateway had two sets of doors, so that parties could be examined and make payment of any toll before being allowed through the second door. The Knag Burn passes under the Wall in a culvert much as it would have done in Roman times, and between the burn and the fort the military way can be seen winding up to its east gate.

Housesteads

Vercovicium: the hilly place
Positioned high on the Whin Sill, in the most scenic of landscapes, is Housesteads. Without doubt it is a true frontier fort. It is listed between the entries for Carrawburgh and Vindolanda in the *Notitia Dignitatum*. To the Romans this fort was Vercovicium; and for nearly 300 years it was to separate the barbaric north from the civilized south. The short, stiff walk to the fort is by a well-worn track past the museum to its west. This museum should be the first stopping point, for it is here that one is given an insight into what life was like on the Wall.

ABOVE: **Knag's Burn Gate, Housesteads.**

BELOW: **Approaching Housesteads.**

The fort's layout, due to the lie of the land, is unorthodox. Its long side lies parallel with Hadrian's Wall, which thus forms its northern defences. To the south, downhill, is the civilian *vicus*. Outside the south gate, among the ruins of the *vicus*, is the so-called Murder House where the skeletons of a woman and a man with a sword in his ribs were found. Most of the remains seen here date from the third and fourth centuries, when it was garrisoned by the first Cohort of Tungrians; later they were reinforced by cavalry regiments from Gaul and Spain.

The main entrance to the fort was by the east gate, the *porta praetorium*, which led directly to the headquarters building. A broken figure of the goddess Victoria found here is believed to have been one of a pair.

ABOVE: **The north gate, Housesteads.**

BELOW: **The latrines, Housesteads.**

North Gate

On a clear day you can see up to 15 miles (25km) from the north gate at Housesteads, which gave the soldiers in the fort ample time to prepare against marauders. At one time the gate had a causeway leading up to it, but this was removed during excavations to expose the foundations. The gateway, like all others at Housesteads, has twin portals divided by piers, both of which are still standing. To the west of the north gate are the remains of turret 36b. This was demolished in 124 when the order was given to place forts on the Wall itself. From the positioning of this turret it can be seen that the Wall was originally designed to run to the rear of the Whin Sill, away from the edge.

Latrines

In their public health the Romans were unsurpassed; today nearly half the world's population has less access to clean water than did the inhabitants of Ancient Rome.

Although ignorant of the dangers of bacteria, the Romans did understand sanitation. Situated in the south-east corner of the fort is the multi-seated latrine; an ingenious drainage system allowed it to flush the waste out into a sewer, as well as providing water for the sponges that were used in place of toilet paper. It is from the stone containers that held these sponges that the expression 'don't get hold of the wrong end of the stick' originated. The paved central island was the entry and the wooden latrines were suspended over the large channels.

Commandant's House

Between the south gate and the *principia* lie the remains of the commanding officer's house. The house was first built in an 'L' shape; later, it was extended to become a courtyard house with a tiled roof, the few windows of the inner atrium offering protection from the harsh winds here. Similar to the hospital (*see* below) in plan, it covers a larger area than any other building in the fort, but because it was on steep ground it had to be terraced.

Comandant's house, Housesteads.

Headquarters Building

Sited centrally between the east and west gates of the fort is the headquarters building, which dates from the Severan age (193–235). It was here that the administration for the fort was done and the standards stored. The building is in three parts, which are not always easy to define because of the poorly preserved eastern end. Entering the building from the *via principalis*, we pass through what remains of the flagged courtyard and set foot in a cross hall where the column bases of a colonnade are still visible. The cross hall, or *basilica*, was the assembly hall and had a raised platform in its north-west corner; it was from here that the commander issued orders. Leading off from the cross hall is a row of five rooms: the central room was the official shrine of the Emperor and the place where the standards were kept.

Headquarters building at Housesteads.

Hospital

Adjacent to the *principia* is the *valtudinarium*: the hospital. Once again this was a courtyard building made up of small rooms arranged round a central courtyard, in which herbs to treat the sick may have been grown. Most forts had hospitals and the physicians who worked there had distinct titles. In times of battle special soldiers were assigned to collect the wounded and take them to a first-aid station; these men were paid by the number of wounded they retrieved.

The Granaries

In Roman times the most important food was corn, and buildings devoted to its storage had to meet certain demands. They had to have easy access with adequate space for loading and unloading, and this dictated where a granary was sited. Tacitus, writing shortly

Hospital building, Housesteads.

before the Wall was constructed, said that forts should contain sufficient supplies to last a year. To the Romans the granaries, known as *horrea* or buildings for storing food, were part of everyday life. Built on high ground, their floors were raised to help keep whatever was stored dry; ventilation was by vents set in the exterior walls. The entrances to the granaries at Housesteads are at the west end of the building, raised up like loading bays. Access was by the west gate, which reduced the congestion on the *via principalis*. Whether or not there was an upper floor is uncertain, but the buttressed outer walls were strong enough to have supported one.

Housesteads granaries.

West Gate

The west gate was where the supply wagons arrived on their way to the granary and workshops. Anyone with business at the fort would have to state their business and present their credentials to the sentry who manned the gate; they would then proceed to the guardroom to check that the paperwork was in order. The western sector of the fort was taken up with the barrack blocks, none of which remain. This gateway is the best preserved, its northern side standing to its full height.

TOP: **The west gate, Housesteads.**

BELOW: **The south gate, Housesteads.**

South Gate

The fort is best seen by entering the south gate and then walking uphill on the *via principalis*. Used primarily by civilians, this gate led from the *vicus* through to the north gate. The two arched entrances that stood here were at one time supported by stone piers. In contrast to the smaller stone of the curtain wall, these arches were built with large squared blocks. Flanking the gate was a pair of guardchambers that had towers. The double gates, which were hung on turning posts, pivoted in iron-shod sockets at the bottom edge.

Milecastle 37

The word 'milecastle' first came into use in 1708 when Robert Smith noted that it was a term used by people who lived local to the Wall. Regularly spaced at every Roman mile, they acted as bases for small units. Of the eighty that were built only fifty-eight have been located, and of these only six have been fully excavated. Their function was unclear as the double gates were wide enough for wheeled traffic. Built by the *Legio II Augusta*, milecastle 37 is situated on the crest of House-steads Crags and contains the remains of a small barracks. Excavated in 1853 by John Clayton, it is one of the best-preserved examples on the Wall.

The North Gate

The north gateway, excavated in 1989, shows evidence that it has been blocked and partly demolished. An oddity about this gate is that it could have been of little use as it leads directly to a 200ft (60m) drop; this is possibly why it was narrowed before being blocked.

TOP: **Milecastle 37.**

BOTTOM: **Milecastle 37's north gate.**

Cuddy's Crags.

Cuddy's Crag

Cuddy's Crag is a name derived from St Cuthbert, and from its summit the views are magnificent. Housesteads and Sewingshields Crags rise to the east, Broomlee Lough lies beneath, Greenlee Lough to the north and Crag Lough to the west. These places are the haunts of water birds and occasionally geese. Small farmsteads are scattered across the landscape and the tenacious rowan tree can be found clinging like limpets to the crag.

Rapishaw Gap.

Rapishaw Gap

The Wall disappears on the brink of Rapishaw Gap, then reappears on the slopes of Hotbank Crags, with its fine view of the Northumberland lakes. The largest is Greenlee Lough, bounded on its south side by the high and steep rocky cliff of Hotbank. This is one of the places where the white water lily grows wild, and in winter months is the haunt of swans. It is also the crossing point of the Pennine Way.

Crag Lough

Crag Lough glimmers along the foot of the crags at Hot Bank, beyond which the Wall climbs away again, frequently on the edge, towards Sycamore Gap and the summit of Whinshields.

The view from the summit of Hot Bank Crags is magnificent. The nineteenth-century writer Collingwood Bruce has this to say; 'The view from the summit is very extensive and fine. All the four loughs Broomlee, Greenlee, Lough and Grindon are in sight. The temporary camp at West Hotbank, near the large quarries on the ridge to the north, will suggest that the Romans also exploited this source of good stone. Beyond the waste to the north-east lie the Simonside Hills, and beyond them is the Cheviot range. The heather-clad hill immediately to the south of us is Barcombe, from which the Romans procured some of their stone. The defile leading by its western flank to the South Tyne will be noticed, and the wisdom of guarding it by a permanent fort perceived. The platform of this fort at Chesterholm may be distinguished by its peculiarly verdant surface. On the south side of the Tyne, Langley Castle may be observed, near the angle of a large plantation; beyond it are the chimneys of the disused smelt-mills. The valley of the river Allen is seen joining that of the Tyne; and a little above the confluence of the two rivers, the ruins of Staward pele, on the east side of the Allen, may be discerned. In the distance, to the south-west of us, are the lofty summits of Cross Fell and Cold Fell, with Skiddaw and Saddleback emerging from far behind them.'

Crag Lough.

Highshield Crags

The crag, which forms part of the Whin Sill, is impressively situated above the lough that gives it its name. It is the smallest but by far the prettiest of the lakes, and the basalt cliffs rising sheer from its waters are reflected in its surface. Boggy ground lines the eastern and southern shores.

Sycamore Gap

The aptly named Sycamore Gap lies in a dip in the Wall, just west of milecastle 38 and before we reach Steel Rigg. Erected on stepped foundations and keeping its horizontal coursing, the Wall takes a dive into the gap more impressive than at Thorny Doors (*see* below). Ever since it appeared in film *Robin Hood Prince of Thieves* this tree has been known as the Robin Hood tree. When, in the preceding scene, Kevin Costner stood on the beach at Dover and uttered those memorable words to Morgan Freeman 'Come Hazeem, by nightfall we will celebrate with my father in Nottingham' he failed to say they would be going via Hadrian's Wall. Quite what he was doing here, so far from home, is known only to Hollywood. As the crow flies, Nottingham lies 160 miles (260km) to the south!

LEFT: **Highshield Crags.**

BELOW: **Sycamore Gap.**

Milecastle 39, Castle Nick.

Milecastle 39

From Sycamore Gap the Wall ascends steeply to the summit of Peel Crags, then descends to the milecastle known as Castle Nick. The milecastle is so-called because of its location in one of the Whin Sill's 'nicks'. Unlike milecastle 37, Castle Nick is longer north to south than it is east to west. It has been excavated a number of times over the years and the foundations of a small barrack block are still to be seen within its walls. Pottery found on the site show that it was occupied continuously until the fourth century.

Peel Crags

At the western end of Crag Lough we have Peel Crags. Popular with climbers, this north-facing crag can be reached in a short twenty-minute walk from the car park at Steel Rigg. In late spring the sound of the curlew and skylark can be heard. The crag, which is dolerite, forms part of the Whin Sill and is impressively situated above the lough. In winter the frictionless nature of the rock makes climbing an experience to remember. At the base of the crag, situated in a blind gap, is a supernumerary turret. Built after the Wall was completed, it is generally assumed that it was there to prevent people slipping through the Wall unobserved at this point.

Peel Crags and wall.

Ascent from Steel Rigg.

Whinshields Crags

From Steel Rigg the path gently climbs the great Whin Sill until it reaches its highest point on the Wall at Whinshields Crags. The ascent will take twenty minutes and from the mid-point we can look back and see quite clearly the Wall ditch running down the eastern slope of the crags.

The Summit

On a clear day the view stretches from the north Pennines to Bowness-on-Solway and the Border forests. The path then descends to the amusingly named Bogle Hole, down through Thorny Doors; from here it is a gentle stroll up to Cawfields Crags.

Windshields Summit.

Thorny Doors

Descending from the Winshields, the path falls first to the Bogle Hole, and then Caw Gap. After crossing the gap we pass what remains of turret 41a to reach Thorny Doors, which is another break through the crags. In the dip you can pass through the iron gate to view a section that is fourteen courses in height; nowhere else is higher on the whole Wall, since Hare Hill was largely rebuilt in the nineteenth century. So steep is the slope that the Wall is stepped here and its courses laid at right angles to the lie of the land. It was here, close to the foot of the cliffs that a building stone similar to that of a centurial stone was found; it commemorated work done by the tribe of the Durotriges of Dorset.

Thorny Doors, east of Cawfields.

Cawfields

At Cawfields the wild and beautiful land-scape resounds to the plaintive cry of the curlew. Milecastle 42, built on a slope at the edge of the escarpment known as the Whin Sill, is one of the best preserved on the Wall. How wheeled traffic ever accessed its gateways is hard to imagine, but the plan called for a milecastle, and regardless of the practical problems it was built. A puzzling fact to be found here is that only the north wall and its gate were built to the Broad Wall specification. The remainder of the milecastle and the Wall on either side was built to Narrow Wall measurements – it abuts the north Wall without being bonded in. It was built to house between twenty and thirty men, and the only significant find was a dedication slab showing that it had been built on the orders of Hadrian, by Platorius Nepos.

The Vallum, once thought to have been a much older frontier line built by Severus, was built by Hadrian. Laid out in the same way that they built roads, it ran from point to point and formed what has been described as a 'flexible line made up of straight pieces'. The strip of land that lay between the Wall and Vallum was strictly controlled. At Cawfields, stone flagging supported its turf sides and the berms of the Vallum are wider on the south than the north. To the south of the milecastle is one of the most impressive lengths of Vallum that can be seen.

Cawfields milecastle.

Vallum at Cawfields.

Cawfields Quarry

Beyond the milecastle a great slice of the Wall has disappeared because of quarrying. Further damage to the Wall was prevented by the government when it stepped in and paid compensation to landowners. The area around the quarry pool is now a pleasant picnic site maintained by the Northumberland National Park.

Cawfields Quarry.

Great Chesters, altar stone at the south gateway.

Great Chesters

Aesica
Lying approximately 40 miles (60km) west of Newcastle is the Roman fort of Great Chesters. The Romans called it Aesica, and it is found in the *Notitia Dignitatum* between the entries for Vindolanda and Magnis. Only 3.4 acres (1.4ha) in size, the fort at Great Chesters is one of the smallest on the Wall. To the east the Whin Sill escarpment cuts across the landscape and the land falls away towards Cawfields quarry; to the west the rolling landscape takes us to Greenhead and Thirlwall. One of the most interesting features of the fort is the blocking of the west gate. Although it is now obscured under a layer of turf, this is the only fort on the Wall to retain its blocking *in situ*. In the eastern chamber of the south gate stands a large altar with sculptured side panel.

Mucklebank turret remains (44b).

Mucklebank Turret (44b)

Mucklebank Crag is the highest of the 'Nine Nicks of Thirlwall', standing 860ft (260m) above sea level. At a point where the Wall makes a left turn on its descent to Walltown Nick stands turret 44b; its north and west sides are recessed into the Wall because of the angle. Excavated in 1892, the turret was left open to allow access to visitors. During the excavation a coin from the reign of Valentinian II and a centurial stone were found.

Walltown Crags

Just after the old quarry lies turret 45a, which was built before the Wall as a free-standing signal station similar to the one at Pike Hill (*see* below). Across all of this section the Wall clings to the edge using the sheer north face as added protection. This is one of the many stretches of the Wall where you can walk and enjoy both the Wall and the beautiful views to the north and south.

The 'nick' at Walltown is wide and the Wall runs across it in a straight line. In the middle of the gap, close behind the Wall, is King Arthur's Well. Hutchinson, in his *History of Northumberland*, tells us that this is where Paulinus baptised King Egbert; he probably meant Edwin, King of Northumberland, but Edwin was christened at York, so the story would seem to be untrue. In many places where the Wall climbs steeply up a slope we can see examples of the stone running horizontal, reminding us that the rampart walk must also have been stepped at these points.

Turret 45a, Walltown Crags.

The Wall west of turret 45a at Walltown Crags.

Thirlwall Castle.

her animals may have caused; she then had to pay a further 20 shillings for inciting a shepherd to burn down a house on the baron's estate.

Like many castles Thirlwall has a ghost story. Legend tells us of a baron of Thirlwall who returned from a Border raid carrying with him a table of solid gold. In time the Scots attacked the castle and the baron was slain along with all of his retainers. The Scots then began their search for the treasure, which was in the care of a mysterious dwarf. In the heat of the fray the dwarf threw himself and the treasure into a well; then, by supernatural power, he drew the top down over himself and his charge. There he remains, still under the influence of the spell, until the son of a widow releases him from it.

Thirlwall Castle

The shattered remains of Thirlwall Castle stand close to the Roman Wall 3½ miles (5.5km) west of Haltwhistle. Entirely built of stones from the nearby Roman station at Magna, this grim stronghold of the Thirlwalls is situated on high ground above the river.

We first hear of Thirlwall in 1255 when it was part of Scotland, its name being derived from 'a breach in the Wall', when the prioress of the nearby nunnery allowed her cattle onto land claimed by the Baron of Thirlwall; their argument was to grow so heated that eventually she challenged him to combat in order to settle the matter once and for all. This was not as funny as it may sound, since it was the custom for the disputants to hire champions to fight for them. The arrangements had almost been made for the tourney when the prioress agreed, against her will, to pay 10 pounds for any damage

Gilsland

Gilsland, a small village that sits uncomfortably astride the Northumberland/Cumbria border was, in Victorian days, a spa town. The River Irthing and its tributary the Poltross Burn define its borders. In the garden of the former vicarage, standing amidst overgrown nettles, is a 200 yard (180m) section of Narrow Wall that sits not only on the Broad Wall foundation but also on three courses of the Broad Wall itself. It would appear that construction of the Broad Wall was in progress when the order came to reduce its width and, rather than demolish it, they carried on building at the new width.

It is a fact worth noting that the only title of nobility ever conferred by Oliver Cromwell was that of Baron of Gilsland, to one Charles Howard.

The Wall at Gilsland.

Poltross Burn milecastle.

Poltross Burn

On the west bank of Poltross Burn stands milecastle 48, otherwise known as 'the King's Stables'. It lies on a steep slope south-west of Gilsland. The name, 'The King's Stables', comes from an old Arthurian legend that tells of it guarding the passage of the Poltross. Calculations made by using what remains of a flight of steps show that the ramparts were 12ft (4m) above ground which, allowing for the hillside, indicates that the external height of the Wall without its parapet was 15 Roman feet. Built by *Legio XX Valeria Victrix*, it is one of only two milecastles to have two barrack blocks. It is one of the best-preserved milecastles on the line of the Wall and is reached via a footpath from the Station Hotel car park.

Willowford

One mile (1.6km) east from Birdoswald is one of the longest and best-preserved sections of the Wall, over ½ mile (800m) in length and standing up to 8ft (2.4m) in height. It was constructed on the foundations of the Broad Wall; as we approach the farm the broad wing-walls of turret 48a can be seen, but by contrast 48b has only an eastern wing-wall, its western side tapering to accommodate the Narrow Wall that lies beyond. This detail suggests that 48b was actually under construction when the order came to reduce its width to align with the change.

At the farm the Wall descends to the flat ground by the river where once there stood an impressive Roman bridge, but because the river has changed its course over the centuries the abutment is now landlocked. The abutment here is less impressive that the one at Chesters and shows that its building was carried out over three periods. The first bridge to be built was the Hadrianic; next, after the stone arches were removed in 140, came the Antonine Bridge. The last phase did not take place until the latter part of the second century, or possibly in the early third century when it carried the military road. It is one of three preserved Roman bridge abutments in Britain, the others being at Piercebridge and Chesters.

The Wall at Willowford.

The abutment at Willowford Bridge.

Harrow Scar

Situated on the west side of the Irthing Gorge at the top of the cliffs known as Harrow Scar is milecastle 49. It was here that the turf Wall ran to the south side of the east gate at Birdoswald. Why the contrasting materials of the curtain to the east and west of the Irthing remains unclear, but it may have been due to the lack of limestone and mortar. However, in 1945 excavations by archaeologists Simpson and Richmond showed that the turf Wall and its ditch were overlain by the fort. It was during the reign of Hadrian that this mile-long (1.6km) section was rebuilt in stone. This is the only site where the turf Wall has been found to follow a different course to its stone successor.

Harrow Scar milecastle.

Birdoswald

Banna: the spur
In a picturesque setting, high above the River Irthing, the fort of Banna is arguably one of the most spectacularly located forts along the line of the Wall; It is also one of the best preserved of the sixteen forts on Hadrian's Wall. The first fort at Birdoswald was constructed of turf and timber for the cavalry. It marked the end of the stone section of Hadrian's Wall that lay to the east and the start of the turf Wall going to the west, and its prime function was to defend the bridging point across the Irthing, a half-mile (800m) to the east at Willowford.

TOP: **Banna; Birdoswald granaries.**

BELOW: **The east gate at Birdoswald.**

The garrisoning of the fort is by no means clear; although designed for cavalry it was to become occupied by the infantry in the second century. Of the buildings that lie within the fort only the granaries and an exercise hall have been excavated. To the south of the fort a *vicus* of timber buildings has been unearthed; it appears to have been constructed mid-way through the third century. In 1959, the fort cemetery was located to the west of the *vicus*.

The east gate is one of the best preserved on the Wall and the first arch stone and impost stone that supported the arch can still be seen.

Leahill Turret (51b)

West of the Irthing the Wall was initially built of turf but the turrets, such as Leahill, continued to be built in stone that was set wholly within the width of the turf Wall. Access was by a doorway in the rear wall and from the Wall walk.

Leahill turret.

Pike Hill Signal Tower

Pike Hill lies on the summit of a ridge with an all-embracing view. The signal tower, or what remains of it, dates from the Trajan period but it was later incorporated into the Wall at an angle. It was superbly sited so that its flaming warnings could be seen as far as Nether Denton Fort, which lay about a mile (1.6km) to the south-east on the Stanegate. West of Nether Denton the course of the Stanegate is not clearly defined and how it reached Boothby, Brampton Old Church and Carlisle is uncertain.

Pike Hill signal tower.

Banks East Turret (52a)

Less than 100 yards (90m) west of Pike Hill stands turret 52a. This is one of the few sites on the Wall that has a lay-by in which to park. The turret, originally constructed of turf, was some years later rebuilt in stone. Today, when only the footings survive, it is difficult to imagine that a two-storey tower some 20ft (6m) high once stood here. By the early third century Banks East, like Piper Sike, Pike Hill and Coesike, had become surplus to requirements and was allowed to fall into ruin.

Banks East turret.

Lanercost Priory.

Lanercost Priory

Standing close to Hadrian's Wall, this beautiful church was built by Augustinian monks using stone from the Wall. It was built in 1166 by Robert de Vaux when it was home to about fifteen canons. However, the Scots who terrorized the north often broke the tranquillity of their lives. In time it grew to be one of the better-off monasteries and flourished up to the Dissolution of the Monasteries by Henry VIII in 1536.

Edward I was to stay here several times when en route to Scotland. The last time was in 1306 when, while on his way to Carlisle, he fell ill and had to rest at Lanercost. For the following six months the Priory was home to 200 people; all had to be housed and fed. Situated near the river, it is a building of great beauty with its nave still being used by the church; the remainder is in the care of English Heritage.

83

Naworth Castle

The first glimpse we have of Naworth is from the Brampton to Newcastle road, with its battlements and towers striking a romantic pose. The grounds are large and the castle impressive. Like Lanercost, it is made up of a great deal of stones from the Roman Wall. This former stronghold of the Wardens of the Marches stands in rugged countryside some 12 miles (20km) north-east of Carlisle.

The most famous figure associated with Naworth is Lord William Howard, or 'Belted Will' as he was known for his habit of wearing a baldrick, or broad belt, which was usually worn as a badge of office by persons of high rank. Scott referred to him in *The Lay of the Last Minstrel* in the following way: 'His bilbao blade, by marchment felt, Hung in a broad and studded belt; Hence in a rude phrase, the borderers still, Called noble Howard, "Belted Will".'

The approach to the castle is through a gatehouse bearing the arms of Dacre.

Naworth Castle.

Site of fort at Castlesteads.

Castlesteads

Camboglanna: winding valley
The small fort that stood at Castlesteads is believed to have been built around the time that the Vallum was built. Lying between the Wall and the Vallum, the fort was unique in being the only fort to be detached from the Wall itself. Inscriptions from the site show that in the second century the fort was garrisoned by the fourth cohort of Gauls and in the third century by the mounted second cohort of Tungrians. In 1791 the gardens of Castlesteads House were redesigned and the site changed beyond recognition.

Stanwix

Uxellodunum: high fort

From Castlesteads the Wall runs for 8 miles (13km) before reaching Stanwix. In Roman times the station here could be seen on a natural platform above the River Eden. When William Hutton arrived in 1801 he tells us that he 'observed a stone in the street, converted into a horse-block, three steps high. With the figure of a man, in a recess, eighteen inches in height, in a Roman dress, and in great preservation.' The fort lay on a ridge of high ground clear of the northern edge of the flood plain. It defended the side of the Wall north of the river, at a point where the course of the Wall moves from the north bank of the River Eden to its south bank. The Roman name for the fort is listed as Uxellodunum, but in the *Notitia Dignitatum* it is referred to as Petriana. Built by *Legio XX Valeria Victrix*, it is the largest fort on the Wall, and for the 800 men of the *Ala Petriana* it was home. The *Ala Petriana*, who came from Gaul, was the largest cohort of auxiliary troops to be stationed in Britain.

Stanwix, Conquest Stone.
(Tullie House Museum)

CHAPTER VI

THE WESTERN TURF WALL: CARLISLE TO BOWNESS ON SOLWAY

The turf Wall was the western counterpart of the stone Wall; it ran from the River Irthing at milecastle 49 (Harrow Scar) to the western end of the Wall at Bowness-on-Solway. It was built during the governorship of Platorius Nepos between the years 122–125; Nepos was the legate Hadrian had charged with the task of building the Wall. Constructed of laid turf blocks cut from the ground adjacent to the Wall, it was 20ft (6m) wide and had an estimated height of 12ft (3.6m) to the parapet walk. At Banks Burn (milecastle 53) the Wall was built with a base layer of cobbles instead of the usual three or four courses of turf blocks. Taking only six months to build instead of the two years needed for a stone wall, it was a stopgap; within a few years stone replaced the turf. Why we have this contrast in materials to the west of the Irthing remains obscure, but it is thought it was due to the lack of limestone for mortar to the west of turret 53b.

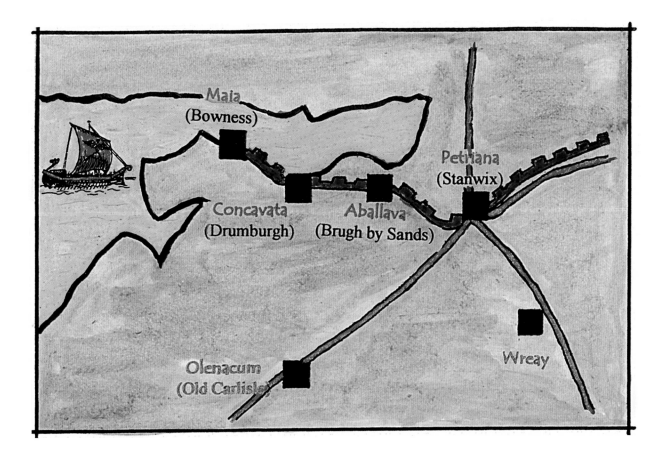

Route of the Turf Wall.

The milecastles along this line of the Wall were built in turf and timber, and as far as is known all but one, High House, was demolished when the Wall was rebuilt in stone.

The western sector was also dangerous, not only for the nature of the ground but also for the sullenness of the people who lived there. Therefore it is no surprise to find the *Ala Petriana* stationed here; they were the only military *Ala* in Britain. From Stanwix the road led through Carlisle to the outpost of Netherby on the Esk, west of Stanwix, which overlooked the river crossing. At Kirkandrews the Wall and Vallum separate. The Vallum goes direct to where the fort stood at Brugh by Sands, whereas the Wall goes north to Beaumont where it turns west.

Beaumont

Dating from the late twelfth century, St Mary's Church at Beaumont stands on the motte of a medieval castle. It was built from the stone taken from the ruins of turret 70a, which lies beneath the church. It is at this point that the Wall, which had been travelling north-westerly to reach Beaumont, returns to its western course to Brugh by Sands.

St Mary's Church site of turret 70A, Beaumont.

Statue of Edward I at Brugh by Sands.

Brugh by Sands

Aballava: the apple orchard

When excavated in 1922, it was found that the eastern gate of the cavalry fort at Aballava was in the south-east corner of the church-yard; the road running through the village is where the *via princi-palis* would have been, while the church stands on the site of the commandant's house. The first known unit at Aballava was in the second century when the First *Ala* of Tungrians garrisoned it; they were followed by the 1,000-strong cavalry regiment called the First Cohort of Nerva's Own Germans.

It is often forgotten that Rome's African provinces were some of its most important; indeed, at some point there may even have been a black emperor. Today, there is archaeological evidence of an African presence at the fort at Brugh by Sands. A fourth-century altar stone found in the village of Beaumont shows that a *numerus* of Aurelian Moors was garrisoned at the fort; confirmation of this unit can be found in the *Notitia Dignitatum*, in which it refers to a

'prefect of the numerus of Aurelian Moors at Aballava'. Marcus Aurelius, in whose honour the unit was named, reigned during a period when the Roman Empire was constantly at war.

The village of Brugh by Sands is known as the place where Edward I died on 7 July 1307, on his way to fight the Scots. While en route to a battle with Robert the Bruce he fell ill with dysentery and died, and his body was brought to this church to lie in state. A window on the south of the church honours his memory; outside the village a monument on the marshes marks the spot where he died.

By the middle of the fourteenth century the Norman castle that once stood here was in ruins; since then it has completely disappeared and in its place stands the fortified church of St Michael. Built almost entirely of stone from the fort, it was erected around 1180. Its western tower, used as a place of refuge from the Border Reivers, has no exterior door, access being via the church.

In the past the village was also known for its horse races, which were held on Brugh Marshes to celebrate the accession of the Earls of Lonsdale; the last occasion on which this occurred was in 1883.

Drumburgh

Concavata: hollowed out/bog of the bitterns

The *Notitia Dignitatum* gives the name of the fort here as Concavata but the Rudge Cup gives the name as 'Coggabata'. Built to guard the fords over the Solway, Drumburgh fort occupied a small knoll that overlooks the flat lands to the east and west. The site lies 4 miles (6½km) west of Brugh by Sands and was linked by a Roman road with Kirkbride. Measuring 2 acres (0.8ha), it is the smallest fort on the Wall and the only force known to have been here is the *Cohors II Lingonum*, a 500-strong part-mounted unit from Upper Germany. When Leland visited the site in the sixteenth century he reported that the Wall had already been heavily robbed to provide for buildings in Drumburgh.

During the reign of Henry VIII, Lord Dacre took the fort apart and had it made into a 'prety pyle for defens of the contery'. The 'pyle' that he built is now the bastle house (fortified farmhouse) that stands at Drumburgh. In 1802 Hutton had this to say:

I am now nine miles from Carlisle, and four from Boulness, the termination of the Wall. The Castle stands upon a rising ground, at the extremity of the mash; and was erected by the Dacres, two hundred years ago, with the materials of the old Castle, and upon the old foundation. Their arms are placed in the front. It is no more than a large, handsome farm-house.

In 1899 an excavation by Haverfield concluded that it was a milecastle, or a fort very similar to a milecastle.

Drumburgh Bastle House.

The estuary at Port Carlisle.

Port Carlisle

Situated 2 miles (3km) to the east of Bowness, this small harbour was developed as a port called Fishers Cross. At one time sailing boats could make their way to the heart of the city of Carlisle by canal from Port Carlisle. The building of the railway viaduct at Bowness caused the deep-water channels of the Solway to silt up and the canal was abandoned; it was drained in 1853. You can still see the decaying oak breakers beside the silted-up quay.

Port Carlisle is also known as being the Cumbrian home of haaf fishing. For more than 1,000 years, from the middle of May to early September, men have tramped across the mudflats of the Solway to stand chest-deep in its ebbing and flooding waters, holding the large wooden netted frames of the haaf net; these are the haaf-netters. Then, as now, their prey was salmon and sea trout. The word 'haaf', derived from the Norse word *hav*, means open sea.

91

Bowness-on-Solway

Maia: the larger

The fort at Bowness stood high on a cliff overlooking the Solway and marked the western terminus of the Wall. Known as Maia, it is the site of the Wall's eightieth milecastle. For some reason its name is not included in the *Notitia Dignitatum*, but appears on the Rudge Cup as 'Mais'. Maia, from where we derive the name of the month of May, is the goddess of spring. She was the eldest and the most beautiful of the seven daughters of Atlas.

The fort occupied just over 7 acres (2.8ha) and was the second largest on the Wall. It lay, due to the lie of the land, with its long side oriented with the shoreline; this was because 'beast-stealers' from Scotland had been known to wade across the Solway at low tide. Over the years the fort's ramparts have been traced by excavation, though nothing remains to be seen today.

Solway Firth.

Mosaic at journey's end, Bowness.

An arbour marks the end of our journey along the Wall. On the floor a Roman-style mosaic shows the wildlife found in the area; it was created from drawings made by the children of Bowness-on-Solway Primary School.

Final Days

Much has been written about the decline and fall of the Roman Empire, and the search for its cause continues. From the time of the conquest in AD43 it has been said that there always was tension from the proud tribes of Britain. The chieftains, resisting the pressure of Roman civilization, were coerced into submission; to preserve their status they would have to adopt Roman values.

By the early fifth century AD most of the Roman Army had left Britain – the legions being needed for the defence of Italy and Rome itself from invading barbarians – and life once again became perilous. For almost four hundred years the country had enjoyed a period of unprecedented peace; now raiding parties from Scotland and Europe were once again making their presence felt. A plea to the emperor for assistance against local incursions went unheeded; the Romans had their hands full with the Visigoths in Rome and the Rhine frontier. The reply received from the emperor in 410 was that the British should 'guard themselves'. The sixth-century monk Gildas made his final plea saying: 'The barbarians are driving us into the sea, and the sea is driving us back to the barbarians; are we to be slaughtered or drowned?' No help was to come as the Roman Empire had imploded; it was no more.

Much of the gracious living was lost as the embrace of Roman culture disappeared over its many provinces. Roman staples such as olives and fish sauce would no longer be part of the diet, and traders who had been looking after the needs of the soldiers would have to find another way to earn a living. Only the Wall would survive undisturbed at their leaving of this small island.

CHAPTER VII

A WAY OF LIFE

Virgil's *Aeneid* is the story of a man who lived 3,000 years ago in the city of Troy. The poem tells of the anger of Juno and the long years spent by Aeneas and the remnants of his people who, after escaping from the sack of Troy, sailed the seas in search of a place to found a new city. After six years, with their boats battered by storms, the small band of Trojans sailed into the mouth of the River Tiber where they set up their camp on its banks. Here they were to fight a bitter battle with the people of Latium that ended only when they formed an alliance with the Latins, enabling Aeneas to found his city of Lavinium; thirty years later his son, Ascanius Iulus, was to leave the city for Alba Longa. It was from these beginnings, and the birth of Romulus and Remus 300 years later, that Rome rose. From its creation in 753BC, Rome was successively a monarchy, a republic and then an empire, its founding forever linked with the story of Romulus and his twin Remus.

According to myth, Mars the god of war seduced the Vestal Virgin Ilia, daughter to the rightful, but deposed, king of Alba Longa. The babes were ordered to die and were taken to the banks of the River Tiber where they were found by a female wolf who suckled and reared them as her own. When they grew up the young brothers restored the throne to its rightful owner and then set out to found their own city. Unable to choose the site, the brothers agreed to decide its position through augury. While Romulus favoured the new city to be built on the Palatine Hill his brother preferred the Aventine Hill, which lay to the south. The signs made by the auguries, however, were in conflict and sibling rivalry between them led to the death of Remus; this left Romulus to become king and founder of the city.

After naming the city Roma, after himself, he went on to create an army and senate. As the city grew in size Romulus sought out the people who could fight to protect it and formed small units called legions; over the centuries these legions were to transform themselves into an unbeatable army. The most celebrated image of this story is the Etruscan statue of the Capitoline wolf with milk-filled teats that stands in Rome. However, Italian archaeologists have since found the cave in which they believe Romulus and Remus were nursed by the she-wolf. Decorated with seashells and marble, the vaulted space lies buried 50ft (15m) inside the Palatine Hill, once the centre of power in imperial Rome.

Life in the Army

The Roman Army was a cosmopolitan force made up from all areas of the empire. There were Tigris boatmen at South Shields, Tungrians at Housesteads, Syrian archers at Cavoran, Moors at Brugh by Sands and Gauls at Vindolanda; the accepted picture that we have of Hadrian's Wall being the last outpost, manned by cold, shivering Italians, is one that is very far from the truth. It is wrong to think of the Roman Army simply as being Romans.

To serve within the military you had to choose one of three services: the legions, the auxiliaries or the fleet. Only the legions were made up of men holding the status of Roman citizen, even if they had been born outside of Italy. In general the nominal strength of each legion was 5,500 highly trained and heavily armed men. Each was under the command of a *legatus legionis* who had received his commission direct from the emperor. These men were the elite of the Roman Army.

The smallest unit in the army was a *contubernium* made up of eight men who shared a tent while on campaign. Each tent had two rooms, one used for sleeping and one for the equipment. Ten *contubernia* (eighty men) made up a century (not a hundred as one might assume), six centuries formed a cohort and ten cohorts made up a legion; but the first cohort was of double strength. Cavalry rode on the sides where they could protect the flanks, and behind the main group were seven units of light troops followed by seven units of reserve.

The backbone of the legion was its centurions, upon whom fell the daunting task of maintaining law and order. With their swagger sticks – the vine-staffs they used to inflict punishment – they were feared by the men they commanded. The age at which recruits were conscripted into the army was eighteen to twenty-two; at that age they were expected to march 20 Roman miles in five hours at normal marching speed, and if need be 24 miles at a faster pace. They were expected to run at the double and take part in weapon training. To keep them on their toes, full-scale manoeuvres would be held. We are told by the first-century historian Josephus Flavius that 'Roman manoeuvres are conducted as energetically as real battles without bloodshed; and real battles are simply manoeuvres at which blood is shed'. We have to remember that the Roman Army was not trained to fight from a static position; it relied on its carefully rehearsed battle formations to scatter forces less disciplined than itself.

In addition to his arms and armour the Roman soldier had to carry an entrenching tool, a saw, an axe, a wicker basket and three days' rations. It's no surprise to hear Josephus comment that 'the Roman infantryman is as heavily laden as a mule'. With its permanent quarters based in a fort, the legion lived and acted as one. Their meals would be taken at the same time each day from a signal given by a bugler. Another blast on the horn would signal the breaking of camp and the baggage train of 640 mules, one mule for every eight legionaries, would be loaded.

The length of service for these men was twenty-five years, and there was always the possibility of re-enlistment. For the centurion, who normally died in service, it became a way of life. His second in

A *contubernium* (eight-man) unit.

95

command, known as an *optio*, received double the pay of an ordinary soldier.

The auxiliary troops of the legion differed from the legionaries in a number of ways. Recruited from the outlying provinces of the empire they were not Roman citizens; citizenship was granted after twenty-five years' service in the army. They would be stationed in a different province from their home. Instead of the heavy armour of the legionary they carried lighter equipment: the Hamians at Carvoran used the Syrian bow; the Dacians at Birdoswald used the curved sword.

These professional soldiers, both legionary and auxiliary, were in combat for only a small part of their working lives; routine duties, both military and non-military, would take up most of their days. First and foremost, however, the Roman soldier was a fighting man and the rigorous training kept him at peak condition, ready for action at any time. Their training included route marches, assault courses, arms drill and practice in building camps and forts, such as those built at Cawthorn in Yorkshire by *Legio IX Hispania* from York.

The personal weapons carried by a legionary were the short-bladed *gladius* sword, a smaller dagger called a *pugio* and the *pilum*, which was a 7ft (2m) throwing spear. For protection he would wear a helmet and various types of body armour. The most common armour was the *lorica segmentata*. Made of iron bands, it was held together by a strapwork of leather, hinges and buckles, with laces at the front and back. Other types of body armour were made of scales wired to the tunic, and shirts of chain-mail. A studded belt, leather knee-breeches, a thick cloak and heavy hob-nailed sandals completed his dress. The rectangular metal-bound shield that he carried gave any additional protection he required.

By the second century the length of service for both legionaries and auxiliaries was fixed at twenty-five years. In the early days of the empire the legions were mainly recruited in Italy, but over the years the pattern changed, and from Hadrian's reign onward Italy contributed less than 1 per cent of the soldiers in its army.

Standards and Insignia

One of the most visual aspects of the Roman Army was its standards: tall poles topped with various insignia and symbols. The standards helped to keep the units together and were a mark of that unit's achievements. The most famous of these was each legion's *aquila*, or eagle standard, used by the army from 104BC onwards. It was carried by an officer known as an *aquilifer*, identified by the animal-skin that he wore on his head. Its loss was a terrible disgrace and often led to the disbandment of the legion itself. In 55BC Julius Caesar described an incident that happened at the start of his first invasion of Britain; it illustrates how fear for the safety of the eagle could drive the Roman soldiers. Having been tracked by the British all the way along the coast, the Romans found themselves unable to get ashore because their boats were too big to beach. Being in deep water, Caesar's troops were hesitant to leave their ships. Suddenly the *aquilifer* of the tenth legion threw himself overboard and, carrying the eagle with him, cried out 'Leap, fellow soldiers, unless you wish to betray your eagle to the enemy. I for my part, will perform my duty to the Republic and to my general.' Without any further hesitation, and fearing everlasting disgrace, his comrades followed him into the water.

The spiritual centre of a camp was the *sacellum*, a consecrated area in which the flags of the legion were stored. On religious festivals they would be brought out and anointed with oil before being decorated with bands of laurel wreaths. One of these days was the *Dies Aquilae Natalis*, the birthday of the *aquila* of the legion; this was the day on which the soldiers would celebrate the anniversary of the founding of the legion.

When following the standard bearer into battle the soldiers would gather around the eagle for their protection; in other words, it was a point of reference for the troops and a personification of their morale. Pliny tells us that in the days of the Republic the legions had five different animals as its standard; the eagle, the wolf, the boar, the horse and the Minotaur. But it was Marius, in his reform of 104BC, who made the eagle the supreme emblem of the legion because of its association with the god Jupiter. Other symbols were either abolished or relegated to a lesser role.

The eagle was not only of tactical importance, but it was also a desired trophy of the enemy. When Augustus Caesar regained the eagles that Crassus had lost to the Parthians in 53BC the event was celebrated by minting special coins.

The aquilifer eagle standard

Standing directly behind the 'first spear' centurion – the most senior centurion of a legion – was the standard bearer of the legion's eagle. His position, one of prestige, ranked him beneath the centurion but above the *optio*. Known as the aquilifer, he was usually a sergeant of outstanding merit and superior in rank to all other standard bearers. The *aquilifer* of the elite Praetorian Guard wore a lion skin rather than the bear or wolf skin worn by the legionary standard bearers.

The signifier wolf-skin helmet

Each century's *signifier* could easily be seen because he wore the skin of a wolf, bear or lion pulled over his helmet; the paws lay over his shoulders so that they could be tied together at the front while the fur hung down his back. The post of *signifer* was quite challenging. Not only did he have to survive combat while being handicapped by his century's standard, but he also had to act as an inspiring example for the other soldiers, his only defence being the small, round cavalry shield that he carried. He also had the cash management of the century to contend with; therefore he needed to be able to write and calculate well.

The vexillarius banner

When a detachment of soldiers was serving away from a legion they marched under a banner known as the *vexillum*. The *vexillarius* took his name from the woven standard he carried, and the *vexillum* designated the unit's type, legion or cohort. Quite often the figure of an animal would decorate the *vexillum* as well. It was suspended from a crossbar flanked on each side with tassels, and a fringe decorated its trailing edge. The predominant background colour seems to have been red. Both infantry and cavalry used this standard.

Eagle standard.

Signifier **wearing wolf skin.**

Vexillarius **(banner).**

Imaginifer **wearing leopard skin.**

Draconarius **(dragon standard).**

carried by a rider the attached cloth tube tail was extended by the wind passing though it. When carried at speed the air that passed through a *draco* head would create a hissing or droning sound; at times whistles would be mounted on to the staff to make the sound more terrifying. The standard of the *draco* was carried by the *draconarius* rider of a cavalry unit.

The first time the *draco* was used by the Romans was in the so-called *Hippica Gymnasia* in the second century AD; these were training exercises devised for the cavalry in which points were scored by strikes on the tail.

The Horns of War

The lituus
One of the most important attributes of the Romans was their ability to adapt ideas and customs from other cultures. The Roman army did not have military bands but they did have war horns: the *lituus*, the *cornu* and *buccina*. Derived from instruments played by the Etruscans and Celts, they were played by musicians who marched at the head of the legion next to the *aquilifer*. In war, because of its shrill note, the *lituus* was used for giving signals of every kind. Shaped like the letter J, it had a total of forty-three variations of sound that could be used to deploy the army. Its main job was to code the general's orders into signals for troops in battle.

The cornu
Just as important as the *lituus* was the *cornu*. The horn, which took the shape of the letter G, curved around the cornicen's body, was almost 11ft (3.4m) long and was braced by a crossbar to provide a

The imaginifer emperor standard
Each legion would have an *imago* carried on a staff at the head of the legion by an *imaginifer*. The *imago* was a metal bust of the emperor in power or the emperor who had raised the Legion, and was carried by the leading cohort. The *imago* was the post first created by Augustus when he became Emperor.

The draconarius dragon standard
It was the horsemen of the steppes, the Sarmatians and Parthians, who originally developed the *draco* as a standard. The 'banner', in the shape of a dragon's head, was hollow and made of metal, and when

The *lituus.*

by the Roman Army varied, but it was their weapons that gave them the advantage over the barbarian. In the days of the Republic and early Roman Empire, the infantry used swords and specialized throwing spears as their main weapon; during the latter days of the Empire most of the infantry had turned to thrusting spears as their main weapon of choice.

The gladius
Gladius is the Latin word for sword and it refers to the short sword of 24in (60cm). Over the years three designs came to be used: the Mainz *gladius*, the Fulham *gladius* and the Pompeii *gladius*, all named after where they have been uncovered by archaeologists;

means of support for its weight. An original instrument unearthed at Pompeii had a length of 10½ft (3.2m) and a diameter of 55in (140cm); its detachable mouthpiece was 7in (18cm) long. The Roman historian Vegetius, writing in his work *De Re Militari*, has this to say:

> The music of the legion consists of trumpets, cornets and *buccinae*. The trumpets sound the charge and retreat. The cornets are used only to regulate the motion of the colours; the trumpets serve when the soldiers are ordered out to any work without the colours; but in time of action, the trumpets and cornets sound together. The *classicum*, which is a particular sound of the *buccina* or horn, is appropriated to the commander-in-chief and is used in the presence of the general, or at the execution of a soldier, as a mark of its being done by his authority. The ordinary guards and outposts are always mounted and relieved by the sound of the trumpet, which also directs the motions on working parties and on field days. The cornets sound whenever the colours are to be struck or planted. These rules must be punctually observed in all exercises and reviews so that the soldiers may be ready to obey them in action without hesitation according to the general's orders either to charge or halt, to pursue the enemy or to retire. For reason will convince us that what is necessary to be performed in the heat of action should constantly be practised in the leisure of peace.

Weapons and Armour

The need for weapons and clothing was a priority in the Roman army, and factories in Gaul and Northern Italy had to be set up to meet the demand. Throughout its long history the equipment used

The *cornicen.*

Centurion with *gladius*.

length. Later, it is believed, this weapon evolved into the sword used by knights in the Middle Ages.

The pugio

A *pugio* was a small dagger used by Roman soldiers and, like other pieces of equipment, it underwent some changes during the first century, although the shape of the hilt remained the same. The *pugio* was made by sandwiching the tang between two pieces of horn or wood, and any decoration would be by the soldier who had made it. It had a large, leaf-shaped blade of some 8–12in (20–30cm) and a width of 2in (5cm); around AD50 a rod tang was introduced that enabled the blade to become narrower.

however, recent excavations have uncovered a fourth version known as the *gladius hispaniensis*, or Spanish sword. The *gladius* was a stabbing weapon rather than one for slashing, and designed for use in close combat.

The spatha

A *spatha* could be any sword, but more often than not it was one of the longer swords that were characteristic of the middle and late Roman Empire. It replaced the *gladius* because it gave the front ranks of the infantry more reach when thrusting. Used by the auxiliaries, this sword measured between 30 and 36in (75–90cm) in

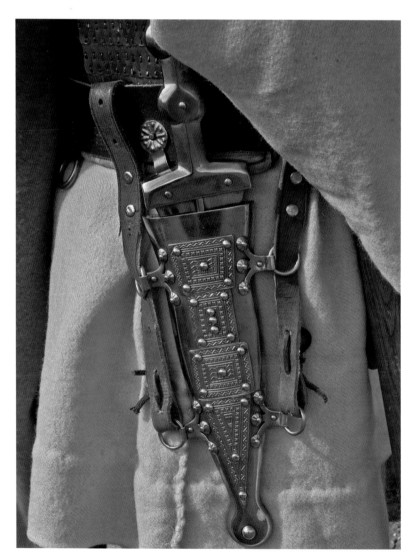

***Pugio* (dagger).**

***Spatha* (long sword).**

Auxiliaries with *hasta* and *pilum*.

allow it to penetrate sufficiently far to hit the person holding the shield. Just over 6ft (1.8m) in length, it weighed between 4 and 8lb (1.8–3.6kg). Its overall range was about 100ft (30m) with a killing range around 60ft (20m). The iron shank was designed to bend on impact so that the enemy could not turn any that were found on the battlefield back on the Romans. Tactics called for the soldier to throw his *pilum* just before charging forward with his *gladius*.

The recurve bow
Tough though it was, the *scutum* (shield) was not enough to stop arrows loosed from the composite bow of the Parthian archers. Lying between north-east Iran and Afghanistan, Parthia was at the edge of the Empire and the Parthian cavalry were noted for their skill at shooting their arrows backwards when riding in retreat. Their final arrow, which gave no time to respond, became known as the 'Parthian shot'. Over the years this action has changed its meaning and today, people who wish to have the last word refer to it as a 'parting shot'.

The historian Plutarch, describing the actions of Crassus at the Battle of Carrhae, in which 30,000 legionaries were either killed or captured, had this to say:

> And when Publius urged the legionaries to charge the enemy horse-men they showed him that that their hands were riveted to their shields (by arrows) and their feet nailed through and through to the ground so that they were helpless.

The recurve bow.

The hasta and pilum
The *hasta* – thrusting spear – was about 6ft (1.8m) in length with a shaft made of ash; its head was made of iron. It was originally carried by soldiers known as *hastati*; later, during the Roman Republic, they were re-armed with the *pila*. They were originally some of the poorest men in the army and could only afford modest equipment, consisting of light armour and a shield. Their usual position was the first battle line, fighting in a *quincunx* formation of five soldiers.

The *pilum*'s design evolved so that it was armour-piercing: its pyramidal head would punch a hole through an enemy shield and

In the peace negotiations that followed, Crassus was seized and executed by pouring molten gold down his throat; this was a mocking gesture to his renowned greed. (Crassus is better remembered as the general who, twenty years previously, had crushed the slave rebellion led by Spartacus.)

The ballista

Originally developed from a Greek siege weapon, the *ballista* was, in effect, a giant crossbow. It was powered by twisted skeins of sinew or hair, and Roman women were known to have grown their hair long as a patriotic gesture. The early *ballistae* were made of wood and held together with iron plates. Its main stand had a slider on the top, into which the missiles were loaded. The slider then passed through the frame of the weapon, which held the rope springs made from animal sinew. Attached to this, at the back, was a pair of winches used to ratchet the bowstring back to the firing position. Drawing back the already taut bowstring provided the energy to fire the missile. When recalling the siege of Jotapata in AD67, Josephus Flavius tells us:

> One of the men standing by the wall, his head was carried away by such a stone, and his skull was flung as far as three furlongs. In the daytime also, a woman with child had her belly so violently struck, as she was just come out of her house, that the infant was carried to the distance of half a furlong, so great was the force of that engine.

The ***tribulus*/caltrop.**

The tribulus

A *tribulus* was a weapon made up of four sharp nails arranged in such a way that, no matter which way it was thrown, one of them was always upright. It was the ancestor of the anti-personnel mine; the sharp point would disable man or beast. It was derived from the caltrop, or foot-trap, and designed to slow down horses and troops. Vegetius wrote in *De Re Militari*:

> The scythed chariots used in war by Antiochus and Mithridates at first terrified the Romans, but they afterwards made a jest of them. As a chariot of this sort does not always meet with plain and level ground, the least obstruction stops it. And if one of the horses be either killed or wounded, it falls into the enemy's hands. The Roman soldiers rendered them useless chiefly by the following contrivance: at the instant the engagement began, they strewed the field of battle with caltrops, and the horses that drew the chariots, running full speed on them, were infallibly destroyed. A caltrop is a machine composed of four spikes or points arranged so that whatever manner it is thrown on the ground, it rests on three and presents the fourth upright.

Lorica segmentata

The *lorica segmentata* was the body armour used by the army throughout the Roman Empire. It was made from broad iron strips attached to leather straps and made in two halves that surrounded the body; additional strips protected the shoulders. During the time of its use it was modified several times; it was used in service until the second century AD.

The ***ballista*.**

Lorica segmentata.

The lorica squamata

This was a form of scale armour used during the days of the Republic. It was made by sewing small metal scales on to a fabric backing cloth. The metal was not very thick but since the scales overlapped in all directions they gave good protection to the wearer.

The lorica hamata

The *lorica hamata* was mail armour worn by both auxiliary and legionary troops. Made from bronze or iron washers, it produced a very flexible form of armour. Although it was labour-intensive to make, taking up to 30,000 rings to make one *lorica hamata*, with good maintenance it would last for several years: the constant friction of the rings kept them from rust.

Lorica squamata.

Lorica hamata.

Helmets

The early Roman army wore helmets similar to those of Greece and Gaul; known as *galea*, they varied greatly in shape. The task of distinguishing the differences is best left to scholars, for archaeologists named them based on their appearance or where they were first unearthed. Originally made of leather, the helmets were strengthened by bronze; later they were beaten out of bronze to afford greater protection to the wearer. The early bronze helmets of the Republican era continued to be in use well into Imperial times. Simple in their bowl-shaped design, they also had added cheek protection. A rear neck guard and front brow guard was added in the early first century and became known as the 'Coolus' style. The helmets of the commanders were surmounted by a crest made from horsehair or feathers, giving them an imposing look and illusion of height. A centurion wore a traverse – side to side – crest, that served as a rallying point during battle.

The cavalry 'sports' helmet, so-called because it was believed that they were used for training, was made up of two parts: a mask that covered the face and a helm to protect the head. Worn by the Batavi, a tribe that provided feared auxiliary forces for the army, they took 200 hours to make and each was tailored to its wearer. For the enemy, a Batavi cavalryman, high on his horse with the metal visor drawn over his face, would have been a fearful sight in battle.

In 2007 the remains of a Roman helmet, made up of three large fragments, was found during excavations near Xanten on the Lower Rhine and sent to the Rheinischen Landes Museum in Bonn for

Scutum.

Scutum

Scutum is the Latin word for shield, and Roman shields came in many shapes and sizes. The classic curved rectangular shape was used through to the third century, when it was superseded by the flat, oval shield of the Imperial era. They were made from three layers of thin wood glued together and covered with leather; the edges were in bronze. An iron or bronze boss protected the handgrip in the centre of the shield. The shields' shape allowed legionaries to overlap them and provide an effective 'shield wall' against missiles.

Sports helmet and face mask.

restoration. It was there that Frank Willer, the museum's chief restorer, made a remarkable discovery: the Romans knew how to make a type of 'super glue'. Willer found traces of the glue by accident while he was removing a sample of metal from the helmet. He was amazed to discover that, after 2,000 years, it had not lost any of its bonding properties.

The Roman Triumph

From the beginning of the Republic to the fall of the Roman Empire, a *triumphus* (triumph) was the crowning moment for a Roman general; it was the summit of his military career. A triumph was a ceremonial occasion given to a victorious general in celebration of a great victory. Once it was agreed by the Senate, he would be allowed to enter Rome in triumph. The display would then proceed in the following order. Heading the procession were the magistrates followed by the Senate. Behind them were the trumpeters to announce the arrival of the *Imperator*, as the victorious general was known. Carts filled with the spoils of war would then pass by, followed by more musicians. White bulls and oxen for sacrifice would be next, then the vanquished army and its leaders, together with any slaves. Following them were the *lictors* (bodyguards) of the *Imperator*, carrying ceremonial *fasces* (bundles of branches)

Auxiliaries' helmets.

The Arch of Constantine.

wreathed in laurel. Then came the *Imperator* riding in a circular chariot drawn by four horses. Dressed in a gold-embroidered robe, he held a laurel bough in his right hand and sceptre in his left; a slave held a crown of laurel over his head, which he would offer to the gods as a sign that he had no intentions of becoming King of Rome. His face would be painted with an orange red pigment to imitate the faces of the statues of Mars, the god of war, or Jupiter, the king of the gods. The sons of the general would walk behind the chariot, as well as his army carrying spears hung with laurel.

The route for the procession was fixed and ran from the Field of Mars to the Circus Maximus and Via Sacra. After passing in state along the Via Sacra, the general would ascend the Capitol to offer sacrifice in the Temple of Jupiter. On the route taken by triumphal processions the Arch of Constantine is the largest of only three such arches to survive in Rome today, and is located between the Colosseum and Palatine Hill.

Money

Roman coins, like those of the Greeks, were based on the universally accepted value of work animals. In Rome the basic unit of currency was the copper coin called an *as*; in Greece it was the silver Drachma. The *as* contained a pound (450g) of copper, but it was diminished from time to time until it contained only 1/24 of a pound (20g). Whatever its weight, an *as* was divided into twelve *unciae*. A *sestertius* was a silver coin originally worth 2½ *asses*; but its revaluation in 118BC took it to four.

The coin that was to become the backbone of the Roman economy for five centuries was the *denarius*. First struck in 211BC it was valued at sixteen *asses*. Prices were variable, depending on the availability of goods and other factors: eight *sestertii* would buy you food for a month. Suetonius tells of Caligula spending 2,700,000,000 *sestercii* in less than a year.

From the time of Gaius Marius legionaries received 225 *denarii* a year; this rate of pay was to remain unchanged for almost 100 years until the reforms brought in by Domitian increased it to 300 *denarii*. In spite of inflation it was another fifty years before a further increase took place. In the second century Septimius Severus increased it to 500 *denarii* and a year later, under Caracalla, this was increased to 675 *denarii*. However, a legionary's pay would be supplemented by the booty taken in a campaign; and from the reign of Augustus all soldiers received 3,000 *denarii* and a plot of farmland on which to retire.

Another coin in circulation at the time was the shekel of Tyre. Few coins make as many appearances in the Bible, the most famous being the thirty pieces of silver given to Judas in exchange for betraying Jesus to the authorities. At that time all Jewish men were required to pay the Jerusalem Temple one shekel per year as their annual tax.

Symbols of Good Luck

All along the Wall you will see the phallic symbol. These were not lewd symbols to the Romans, rather they were common good luck charms; often they were found inscribed on street corners. The phallic inscrip-

Roman purse.

Phallic carving at Chesters.

tion on a doorpost was a charm to ward off bad luck. In ancient Rome, people were of the belief that phallic charms and ornaments would protect them against the evil eye. Before they reached manhood Roman boys would wear a *bulla*, a neck chain with a pouch containing protective amulets – quite often they were phallic symbols. Some also wore a small gold ring with a phallic symbol for luck.

Clothing

The production of clothing was just as important as that of arms, and the same factories turned out thousands of tunics, cloaks and blankets each year.

In the army two types of cloak were in use, the *sagum* and the *paenula*. The most common was the *sagum*, a simple rectangle of heavy wool that reached to the knees and fastened at the throat with a brooch. Made from unwashed wool, its natural oils would make it waterproof; it would also double as the soldier's bedroll when on campaign.

Braccae, the Latin term for trousers, is a style of pants made from wool that became popular with soldiers in the colder climes of the Empire. Fastened with a drawstring, they were of varying lengths from just below the knee to the ankles.

The military boot worn by legionaries and auxiliaries alike was the *caliga*. At first glance they look like sandals, but their three-part construction made them considerably sturdier. Straps, or laces, ensured a snug fit. On certain types of terrain their heavily studded

sole would make them lethal for the wearer. Josephus tells us of a centurion chasing his quarry across the Temple Court in Jerusalem when the metal studs of his boots cause him to slip on the flagstone and fall. The hunter then became the hunted, and was murdered where he fell.

For civilians the basic types of footwear worn changed very little from the foundation of the Roman Republic in 509BC to its fall in

Cloak and brooch.

***Braccae* (trousers).**

Hobnail boots.

Civilian footwear.

476, although the styles did change. Before Hadrian, footwear was plain, but the rise of the Empire saw a growth in wealth and footwear became more ornate. The basic outdoor shoe, which covered the entire foot, was known as the *calceus* and was closed with leather thongs. A slightly lighter shoe was the *crepida*, which covered the back and side of the foot and could be made in several styles. As with forms of clothing the Romans used differences in footwear style to indicate the status of the wearer. Senators, who made the laws in Rome, wore a special form of *calceus* secured with four black thongs, while the Emperor wore *calcei* secured with red thongs. Slaves, on the other hand, did not wear anything on their feet. Just as today, a person's footwear tells a lot about them.

The Bath House

'How have you managed to preserve yourself so long and so well?' asked Augustus of Pollio. 'With wine inside and oil outside', responded the old man.

The act of bathing was not unique to Rome. As with many aspects

Binchester bath house.

of their world they borrowed from other cultures, and in this case it was the Greek custom of bathing daily in a small bath house designed to work up a 'good sweat'. The bathing itself was highly ritualistic and because their workday was confined to the morning, the best time to bathe was in the afternoon; if time allowed they would often stay in the baths for several hours. The Emperor Gordian bathed seven times a day in summer and twice in winter, while Emperor Commodus is known to have taken his meals in the bath. However, mixed bathing was not allowed and the women would bathe separately; those who visited in the afternoon were usually women of ill-repute.

The three basics of a Roman bath are a hot room (*caldarium*), a warm room (*tepidarium*) and a cold room (*frigidarium*). The price of taking a bath was a quadrans, one of the smallest coins in circulation. In a dressing room the bather would change his clothes before entering the central courtyard where he would exercise, play ball games or socialize with others. Once the exercise was complete he would take a dip in the warm pool before moving on to the hot bath; here he would sweat out the body's impurities. A slave would then massage his body with fragrant oils before scraping off the oil and dirt with a scraper called a strigil. Following this the bather would go back in to the warm room where he would socialize once more. The final stage was to take a dip in the cold pool so that the body was refreshed and left the bather ready to go home and enjoy a relaxing dinner. To bathe in the Roman style, with its open spaces and hot rooms, was an indulgence affordable even for slaves.

It is strange to think that public baths that were commonplace for 400 years disappeared once the Romans left this island: from that point on, bathing was a lost cause. It was not for another 1,500 years, until early in the Victorian age, that it came back into fashion.

Spectacle and Entertainment

'Ave imperator, morituri te salutamus'
(Hail emperor, we who are about to die salute you)

The gladiator's salute

To the Wall soldier entertainment meant having a pair of bone dice in his hand, while in other parts of the country it was the amphitheatre. Designed for events such as drama and blood sports, these theatres could hold up to 6,000 people; eight of them have been found in Britain. On a pot found in Colchester, named gladiators adorn its surface; one of them stands with his index finger raised in surrender. At Hawkedon in Suffolk, a complete gladiator's helmet has been unearthed.

The first gladiators we hear of were those who took part in the funeral rites of the Etruscans. During the ceremony two warriors, known as *bustiarius*, would fight over the grave of the deceased to honour the dead. By offering up the blood of the dead to appease the gods, the deceased would be accompanied through the underworld and into the 'next world' by armed attendants. Traditionally it was a ritual confined to men of the aristocracy, but over the years it lost much of its religious significance. In 73BC, after a slave revolt led by Spartacus, the state assumed greater control of public games. Most gladiators were prisoners of war, slaves or criminals sentenced to the *ludus* (gladiator school). In the first century, when three people out of every five did not live to see their twentieth birthday, the odds of a gladiator surviving any one bout were one in ten, and for more than 600 years they died in their thousands on the floor of the blood-soaked arena.

Despite what Hollywood would have us believe, the 'thumbs up' to spare or 'thumbs down' to kill gesture is not entirely accurate. When a gladiator went down he was allowed to raise one finger, this being a sign of appeal for mercy. If the spectators wished the fighter to be spared they pointed their thumbs down, the signal for the victor to drop his or her sword. At the same time they shouted '*Mitte*'

Those who are about to die...

('Spare him'). On the other hand, if they chose his death, they pressed their thumbs towards their chests, symbolizing a sword through the heart, and yelled '*Nece*' ('Cut his throat'). Spectators held the life of the loser in their hands; a wave of their handkerchiefs or a turn of their thumbs decided the outcome.

Again, contrary to what we see in most films, death was less likely to occur than is commonly depicted. Gladiators were expensive to train and replace in the event of their death; keeping the most popular alive was far more practical. A gladiator who survived the arena and lived long enough to retire was presented with a wooden sword.

This sword, known as a *rudis*, was symbolic of the *gladius* and discharged him from service.

Women gladiators were introduced into the arena by Nero in AD63 when he presented combats between women and dwarfs. This practice of having women fight in the arena appears to have been widespread and did not end until 200 when Septimius Severus declared female gladiators illegal because they fought with such enthusiasm.

Although their lives were brutal and short, gladiators enjoyed a good life. They are often seen on mosaics and pottery; at times they were the subject of graffiti. Scrawled on a wall at Pompeii are the words 'Celadus the Thracian, thrice victor and thrice crowned, makes all the girls sigh'. Tertullianus (160–225) said of the games

'This class of public entertainment has passed from being a compliment to the dead to being a compliment to the living.'

Marriage and Divorce

In 17BC Augustus addressed the Senate in the following way:

If we could survive without a wife, Citizens of Rome, all of us would do without that nuisance, but since nature has so decreed that we cannot manage comfortably with them, nor live in any way without them, we must plan for our lasting preservation rather than for our temporary pleasure.

Wedding party.

Because of male dominance, independence was withheld from women in the Roman Empire and their lives were ruled by their fathers and then husbands. It was a time when marriage was seen as an alliance between two families rather than a romance between two people. The minimum age for a girl to be married was twelve, which was soon after she had reached puberty, but the marriage was not regarded as having been fully consummated until the birth of the first child. To the Romans marriage was about procreation and nothing else.

There were two types of marriage observed by Rome. First there was the more formal, legally binding ceremony of the upper classes, and then there was the less formal ceremony that applied to non-citizens. Class was important and most people never married outside their own class. For non-citizens it was only necessary for a couple to cohabit; in other words, marriage was not the result of a written contract but more of an oral agreement.

The giving of a ring symbolized the event and was, like the wedding ring of today, worn on the third finger of the left hand, as it was the belief at that time that a vein led from here to the heart.

Extramarital affairs have gone on in all ages and in all societies; and while women did not have equality with their husbands in the eyes of the law, they did enjoy an almost equal freedom in society. The lending out of one's wife, and wife swapping, were quite common in those days, and Tertullian writes an explicit account of the practice in Chapter 39 of his 'Apology'; in the book he singles out both Socrates and Cato as freely lending out their wives to friends. However, the law looked on the act of adultery, rather than lending, as serious and made it a crime punishable by exile and loss of property. Fathers were permitted to kill their daughters and partners if they were caught in adultery, and husbands were required to divorce an adulterous wife or be prosecuted as a pimp.

Messalina, third wife of the Emperor Claudius, is well remembered for her many affairs. The tale of her sex competition with Scylla, a well-known prostitute, comes from Pliny's *Naturalis Historia*. It was an orgy of sex that lasted all through the night; Messalina won, having bedded twenty-five clients. Tacitus and Suetonius both portray her as a cruel and foolish nymphomaniac.

Food

Napoleon is reputed to have said 'an army marches on its stomach' but he was only repeating what Vegetius had said centuries before. When the Romans arrived in Britain they brought with them a new way of life, new customs, new religion, new food and new ways of cooking. Roman cooking was not all about stuffed dormice; many of the recipes were the basis for today's cuisine. The list of vegetables introduced by the Romans into the British diet is quite lengthy: it includes onions, shallots, leeks, cabbage, peas, celery, turnips, radishes and asparagus. Amongst the herbs were rosemary, thyme, bay, basil and mint. Some of them would be used for medicinal purposes or brewing. However, the degree of difference made to the diet as a whole was dependent upon the social group to which the individual belonged. The Celts, who formed the mass of the population, would have seen fewer changes to their diet for they would not have dined on fine Roman dishes. For them, the introduction of vegetables and herbs would only add variety to their stews.

Both Hadrian and Trajan are recorded as grinding and cooking their own rations. The diet of the Romans in Britain was fairly varied. Records show that in peacetime it would be 2–3lb (1–1.5kg) of grain per day, added to which would be olive oil or lard; this would be augmented with wine, salt, cheese and vegetables.

The tablets at Vindolanda mention forty-six different types of foodstuff such as olives, spices, honey and wine. One of the most famous tablets tells of an invitation to a birthday party. It reads:

> Claudia Severa to her Lepidina, greetings, I send you a warm invitation to come to us on September 11th for my birthday celebrations, to make my day more enjoyable by your presence.

The party would have been very similar to today with snacks, drinks and something to nibble. The Roman menu would have included such things as fresh bread, fish, oysters, fish sauce, honey, ham, wine, cheese, olives, and much local fresh produce. An essential element of almost all Roman meals was the use of fish sauce. They used it, together with wine, vinegar, honey and oil, to create a balance of sweet and sour. An advisor to the Emperor Nero, Gaius Petronius was well versed in the matters of extravagance; here is an account of a light dinner he attended in the course of his duties:

> After a generous rubdown with oil we put on our dinner clothes. We were taken into the next room where we found three couches drawn up and a table, very luxuriously laid out, awaiting us. We were invited to take our seats. Immediately, Egyptian slaves came in and poured ice water over our hands. The starters were served. On a large tray stood a donkey made of bronze. On its back were two baskets, one holding green olives, and the other black. On either side were dormice, dipped in honey and rolled in poppy seed. Nearby, on a silver grill, piping hot, lay small sausages. As for wine, we were fairly swimming in it.

However, it wasn't all banquets; a Roman soldier could eat the equivalent of fast food at a *thermopolium*, something like a small wine bar.

Cooking.

There were a number of these hot food shops around the fort where they could pick up some hot sausage, bread, cheese, dates and, of course, wine on the way home.

One Marcus Gavius Apicius, a famed gourmet who lived during the reign of Tiberius in the first century, compiled the oldest collection of recipes known to survive from antiquity. He was in today's terms another Jamie Oliver. The ten books that make up his collection are arranged much like a modern cookery book; that is, list of ingredients and method of cooking. However, it is worth noting that of the 500 recipes given, 400 include a sauce made with *garum*. This was a salty and aromatic fish-based sauce and one of the most popular. In Roman times sauces and marinades were an essential part of their cuisine. The preparation of most sauces began with pulverized spices and herbs, although it is sometimes difficult to determine whether they were fresh or dried. After being ground in a mortar, plums, raisins and nuts could be then added. The addition of liquids to the mixture enabled it to be reduced to increase its sweetness. Other methods of thickening included the addition of egg yolks or egg whites, or the water in which rice had been boiled. However, the Romans did not eat potatoes, tomatoes, peppers, chillies, courgettes or turkeys; all of these come from the New World and were unknown in Europe before the discovery of the Americas.

To give you some idea of the food that Romans ate, here are a couple of recipes from Apicius for you to try.

Fish sauce: garum

Fish sauce, which the Romans called *garum*, was central to their food; without it the many flavours in a dish would become overpowering. The Roman recipe for making *garum* involved mixing fish with herbs. It was then put into a vessel and allowed to ferment in the sun until it formed a liquid, which usually took about a month. Once the fermentation process was complete it was sieved and stored in an earthenware amphora. However, for the uninitiated, *garum* is something of an acquired taste.

Ingredients:
Fatty fish, such as sardines
Dill
Coriander
Fennel
Celery
Mint
Oregano

Method:
In the bottom of a large container place a layer of herbs. On top of this place a layer of fish, then add a layer of salt two fingers high. Repeat the process until the container is full. Let it rest in the sun for seven days. Then stir daily for the next thirty days. The mixture then becomes liquid and should be strained into another container for use as required.

Garum sauce.

Flat bread.

Bread: panis focaccia

In Roman times baking dough on the hearth made the simplest of breads. It was first flattened on a stone, then covered in the glowing embers of a fire where it became *panis focacius*, 'the bread of the hearth'. It was a method handed down by the Etruscans to the Romans. There are only three ingredients: rye flour, water and sea salt. Without yeast it takes longer to prove. Often baked with herbs, cheese and other titbits, this flat bread is an early prototype of our modern-day pizza.

Ingredients:
    ¾ cup of warm water
    3 cups of rye flour
    1 teaspoon of sea salt
    6 tablespoons of olive oil
    3 sprigs of chopped rosemary
    ½ cup of grated Parmesan cheese
    ½ cup of mozzarella cheese
    ½ cup of capers

Method:
Turn the flour, salt and water into a large bowl and knead the dough by hand until smooth. Place the dough into a well-oiled bowl and allow it to rest for half an hour. When the dough has rested, roll it out on a well-floured board and shape accordingly. Push your fingertips into its surface to leave indentations, then drizzle with olive oil. Cut the mozzarella into thin slices and place them on the surface, together with the grated Parmesan. Add rosemary, capers and salt to taste, then place on a hot baking tray and cook for twenty minutes. There are many regional variations on the topping such as basil, olives, mushrooms or onions; however, for the ultimate experience, be sure to serve it warm.

Chicken Broth: Pullum elixum iure sue (serves 4)
In fine weather cooking was done outside in the open air and cooking implements were few and simple. The basic diet of the peasant was made up of 'white meats' or rabbit. This broth, rustic in style, was eaten mainly by the poor.

Ingredients:
1 chicken (jointed)
6 carrots, roughly sliced
2 chopped leeks
2 large onions, sliced
1 stick of celery, sliced
2 to 2½ litres of water
2 tablespoons of olive oil
1 clove of garlic
2 bay leaves
Handful of chopped parsley

Method:
In a large pan brown the pieces of chicken in the oil. Add all the chopped vegetables (carrots, leeks, onions and celery) with enough cold water to cover, and then add the garlic, bay leaves and chopped parsley then leave to simmer for about fifty minutes. Serve with fresh bread.

Sadly, having squandered 100 million *sesterces* on his lavish lifestyle, Apicius was overwhelmed by debt and committed suicide; Pliny tells us 'Apicius, the most gluttonous of all spendthrifts, died because of his appetite.'

Cooking chicken broth.

The Passage of Time

It was not easy for the Romans to keep track on time. In Roman days the passage of time was measured by the length of time it was light, and as the earth made its way around the sun, the hours of daylight changed. The Romans could only be precise about three of the sun's positions: sunrise, midday and sunset; other times of the day had to be estimated by using the length of shadows. Seneca asserted that it was impossible to be sure of the exact hour and it would be easier to get the philosophers to agree to something than to gauge the hour of day.

In 263BC a new tool was introduced to make the measurement of time more accurate: the Greeks had developed a variation of the water clock. The *clepsydra*, as it was called, consisted of four major parts: a vessel for providing a constant supply of water, a valve for adjusting the flow of water into the vessel, a reservoir, and a notched flotation rod and a circular face. At high noon the canister would be filled with water until the clock hand pointed to the 12 o'clock position. The water valve would then be opened to allow the water to drip out. As the water flowed from the canister the float would drop, causing the chain that was hooked to the float to move the clock hand. At noon the following day the clock would be checked to ensure that the hand was in the 12 o'clock position. If the pointer had not reached this position the valve would be adjusted and checked every twenty-four hours until it did.

The Antikythera mechanism

In 1901 sponge divers were diving on an ancient Roman merchant ship that had sunk off Antikythera, an island between Crete and the Greek mainland. Unknowingly they brought to the surface an object that hadn't seen the light of day since before the birth of Christ. Its recovery from the sea is thought to have been the beginning of underwater archaeology. Housed in a wooden box, the instrument was made up of a collection of bronze gears that are remarkable for their miniaturization. The mechanism had three dials, one at the front and two at the back. The one at the front, marked with the divisions of the Egyptian calendar (Sothic cycle) had an inner dial marked with the signs of the zodiac. This dial was movable so that it could be adjusted to make up for leap years. During a Sothic cycle of 365 days the start of the year coincides with the helical rising of the star Sirius. The rising occurred shortly after what is known as the Nile flood. At the back a spiral of forty-seven divisions shows the 235-months of the nineteen-year Metonic cycle. As well as calculating the position of the Sun, Moon and other planets, it could determine the timing of an eclipse. The back dial also includes a dial dedicated to the four-year Olympiad cycle that originated in ancient Greece.

Its design is so overwhelming that it has taken some of the highest technology to piece together the mechanism's function and it wasn't until the new millennium that scientists began to unravel its complexity. In 2005 Hewlett Packard photographed the mechanism using an 8-ton X-Tek X-Ray machine. The photographs, in 3D, showed a sophistication that was not thought possible. To date, the Antikythera Mechanism Research Project has accumulated more than one terabyte of data on this instrument alone. What the divers had found, and what it has now been acknowledged as, was an ancient Greek analogue computer. However, the research is far from complete and there is a general belief that the mechanism still hasn't given up all its secrets. The three main fragments of the mechanism that remain can be seen at the Bronze Collection of the National Archaeological Museum in Athens.

The Roman calendar changed several times between the foundation of Rome and the fall of the Empire. Initially it was a lunar calendar made up of ten months starting with the spring equinox; scholars have attributed this calendar to Romulus, the founder of Rome. In 46BC Julius Caesar ordered sweeping changes to bring the calendar back in line with the seasons. One of them was that the year would begin on the first of January, not the spring equinox in March. These changes were to be the basis of the Julian calendar used throughout the Western world up to the introduction of the Gregorian calendar in the sixteenth century.

There were three specific days in each month that had a special name. Based on phases of the moon, these days were probably declared when lunar conditions were right. The reforms made by Numa Pompilius meant that they then occurred on fixed days. The first of these is *Kalends*, which was the name given to the first day of each month. This was the day on which debts were collected; we also get the word 'calendar' from this word. Then we have the *Nones*; depending on the month, this could fall on the fifth or seventh day – traditionally, it was the day of the half moon. Finally we have the *Ides*, the day of the full moon; it comes from the Latin word meaning half division. The *Ides* could be on the thirteenth or fifteenth day, depending on the month. Ever since Titus Spurinna, an Etruscan augur, uttered the immortal words 'Beware the *Ides* of March!' to warn Julius Caesar of the threat to his life, the phrase has forever been imbued with a sense of foreboding. In 44BC, when Caesar reminded him of his dire prophecy, Spurinna replied that the Ides of March may have come but were not yet at an end. An interesting footnote to all of this is that the last Tsar of Russia, Nicholas II, signed his enforced abdication on 15 March 1917.

The thirteenth month

In the sky, the constellations of the zodiac represented the lunar months of the year; on the earth it was a sacred circle of trees. All of us are quite familiar with the twelve signs of the zodiac through the astrology columns of magazines, but what was the thirteenth? Ptolemy gives us the name of this constellation as *Ophicius*, which translates as 'The Serpent Carrier'; in the constellations it lies between Scorpio and Sagittarius. Known as the month of the goddess, the name refers to the bare-breasted female in Sumerian and Minoan cultures holding two snakes. Milton makes a cryptic reference to this sign in his work 'Paradise Lost':

'Satan in likeness of an Angel bright,
Betwixt the Centaure and the Scorpion
stearing…'

Scholars will be delighted to tell you that the Coptic Calendar, which originated three millennia before Christ, has thirteen months.

The passage of time.

119

Religion and Death

With the vast size of the empire, the Romans learned about many new, foreign gods. They did not think that only their gods were those to be worshipped: when they heard of other people's gods, they would regard them simply as gods of which they had not been previously aware. In Rome, religion was in the hands of the state and the Roman attitude to religion was, to say the least, catholic: it allowed everyone to worship his or her own gods. As a result there was not a month in the Roman calendar that did not have a religious festival. The Britons continued to worship their ancestral Celtic deities and the immigrants got on with worshipping theirs, some of which appealed to the British.

The Romans believed that if they appeased their gods, the divinities in return would make their crops fertile, or watch over the family to keep them safe. They also believed that when they angered or disobeyed the gods, retribution would be quick to follow. Each family home would have a small altar and shrine where they would worship every day. The shrine contained statues of the gods and the head of the household led family prayers at the shrine each day. Unlike Christianity, where God is worshipped out of love, the Romans worshipped their gods out of fear.

The worship of the dead was another of the family religious practices. Whenever a person died they were worshipped as a god so that the family would not be haunted. The Romans believed that the souls of the dead would travel to the underworld by way of the River Styx. To ensure the safe passage of their soul, a coin was placed into the mouth of the dead to pay Charon, the boatman of the underworld. It was beliefs such as these that brought them into conflict with the new religion of Christianity. Death in the Roman world was viewed as a spectacle, from the tragic death of Lucretia, whose rape and subsequent suicide led to the collapse of the Roman monarchy, to Agrippina, who was poisoned by her own son Nero. At times the manner in which a person died was the most telling indication of their true character. Over the years many of Rome's memorable people have had their last words written down for posterity. Who has not heard that epitome of betrayal used by Shakespeare, '*Et tu Brute?*' These words refer to a rumour spread by Servilia, Brutus's mother and Caesar's mistress, that Brutus was his natural son.

Mithras (Museum of Antiquities).

SITES TO VISIT

The sites are listed here travelling east to west. Sites marked *** are under the management of English Heritage.

South Shields: Arbeia Roman Fort
Remains of fort that show its original outline along with several buildings, including a full-size reconstruction of the west gate. Also reconstructed is the *praetorium*, the commanding officer's house. There is a small but interesting museum with a variety of artefacts on display.

Wallsend: Segedunum Roman Fort
The Segedunum Museum and Visitor Centre at Wallsend is a 'must-see' for anyone with an interest in Hadrian's Wall. The 100ft (30m) viewing tower gives a superb view of the site, which also includes the only reconstructed bath house in Britain. Within the viewing tower are a number of galleries as well as a computer animation showing life at Segedunum through the ages.

Newcastle
There are traces of the fort buildings within the castle keep area.

Museum of Antiquities, Newcastle
The first thing to see in Newcastle if you are seriously interested in what the Romans did in the north. Its Roman collection is the most impressive outside London. For hundreds of years it was thought that the Wall was the work of Septimus Severus; that was until a stone from milecastle 38 was found recording the work to have been done in Hadrian's reign. Also on display is a full-length scale model of Hadrian's Wall.

Benwell: Temple and Vallum Crossing***
At Benwell the remains of a small temple can be found at Broomridge Avenue, and part of the causeway over the Vallum can be seen a little to the west at Denhill Park.

Denton Turret***
A short stretch of Wall and remains of turret 7b.

Heddon-on-the-Wall***
A 300-yard (270m) stretch of Wall up to 6ft (1.8m) thick in places.

Corbridge Site***
This was a supply base for Hadrian's Wall. The remains of a forum, granaries, workshops and other building can be seen. There is also a large museum displaying the many finds on the site.

Planetrees***
A short stretch of Wall showing the change from Broad Wall to Narrow Wall.

Brunton Turret***
One of the best-preserved turrets on the Wall. There is also a 70-yard (64m) section of the Wall here.

Chesters Bridge Abutment***
The remains of the east abutment of the Roman bridge that stood here carrying the Wall across the River Tyne.

Chesters Fort***
A cavalry fort built across the line of the Wall to house the *ala milliariae*. It is the best-preserved cavalry fort in Britain. The visible remains of the fort include all six gateways and two interval towers in its southern defences. Also to be seen are the *principia* and *praetorium* with its own central heating and private bath house. The public bath house at Chesters has been acclaimed as being the most impressive example of a bath house in the whole of the Roman Empire. The site museum contains Roman sculptures, inscriptions and altars that have been collected over the length of the Wall.

Limestone Corner***

Standing on an outcrop of whinstone, the Vallum at Limestone corner shows some of the difficulties experienced by the Romans when building the Wall.

Carrawburgh***

The remains of small temple dedicated to Mithras can be found close to the road, outside the earthworks of a fort.

Sewingshields Crag***

A well-preserved 2-mile (3km) stretch of Wall that takes in milecastles 34 and 35 before reaching Housesteads.

Housesteads Fort

Standing high on the Whin Sill, Housesteads is the most dramatic and scenic of forts. It is an open site where people can wander at will. Barrack blocks, hospital, latrines and commandant's house are all to be seen here. There is also a visitors' centre and small museum. The National Trust and English Heritage jointly manage the site.

Once Brewed

Visitor centre managed by the National Park Authority. It displays the Wall landscape and wildlife that can be seen here.

Vindolanda

Everything expected of a Roman site can be found here at the fort of Chesterholm. Managed jointly by the Vindolanda Trust and English Heritage, the consolidated remains together with the reconstructed fort make it one of the most visited sites in the country. It also has a museum with a major collection of artefacts from the site.

Sycamore Gap

Lying between Housesteads and Steel Rigg, Sycamore Gap became famous when it featured in the opening sequence of Kevin Costner's film *Robin Hood: Prince of Thieves*. The tree here has probably been photographed more than the Wall west of Housesteads.

Whinshields Crags***

Rising to 1,230ft (375m) above sea level, this is the highest point on the Wall. From here the Northumberland landscape unfolds in all its glory.

Cawfields***

A stretch of Wall that features both milecastle and fort turret, 41a and 42.

Walltown Crags***

Standing less than half a mile (800m) north of the Roman Army Museum at Carvoran is Walltown Crags. With 400 yards (370m) of Wall snaking over the landscape, it is one of the best places to view the Wall.

Carvoran: Roman Army Museum

History comes alive at this spacious museum. There are displays of what life was like for a Roman soldier on the Wall, full-size figures and a short film titled 'Following the Eagle' to guide you around the site.

Poltross Burn Milecastle***

Milecastle 48, situated to the south-west of Gisland, is one of the best-preserved milecastles on the entire length of Hadrian's Wall. Remains of the north and south gates, enclosing walls, barrack blocks and other buildings are clearly discernable.

Willowford***

At Willowford, just west of the village of Gilsland, stand the impressive remains of the eastern abutment of the bridge used by Hadrian. The abutment is well preserved and has informative signs to show how the bridge looked in Roman times. This also is an English Heritage site.

Birdoswald

Just west of Willowford lies Birdoswald, and it is here that you can see the early turf Wall built in 122. The best-preserved areas are the granaries and gates. In the visitor centre you can see displays that tell the history of the fort throughout its history.

Carlisle, Tullie House Museum

The museum houses various finds, which have been discovered from sites at the west end of the Wall.

GLOSSARY

Ala   Unit of auxiliary cavalry, usually around 500 men.

Amphitheatre   An oval arena with banks of seats on all sides, used for gladiatorial performances.

Amphora   A large, two-handed vessel for the storage of wine or olive oil.

Apicius   Marcus Gavius Apicius, a first-century Roman nobleman credited with writing the first book of recipes, *De Re Culinaria*.

Aquilifer   A trusted veteran of twenty years who carried the Eagle Standard.

Ashlar   Hewn and squared stone laid in courses.

Auxiliaries   Non-citizen troops in a unit other than a legion who garrisoned Hadrian's Wall; included both infantry and cavalry soldiers.

Auxiliary Unit   Comprised of both legionary and auxiliary troops, it was either all infantry, all cavalry or a mixture of each. The units were divided into centuries (eighty men), each in the charge of a centurion.

As   A small copper coin.

Barbarian   A Greek term adopted by the Romans to describe foreigners or non-Romans.

Ballista   A military siege weapon for hurling missiles into enemy fortifications.

Broad Wall   The gauge of Hadrian's Wall when built first: around 10ft (3m) thick.

Caldarium   Hot room in a bath house.

Caligae   A hob-nailed heavy leather sandal worn by the Roman Army.

Centuria   A century of infantry soldiers usually comprised of 80–100 men commanded by a centurion. A century could be accommodated in a single barrack block.

Cohort   Unit name for auxiliary troops; either all infantry, all cavalry or a mixture of both (usually 500 or 1,000 men).

Commanding Officer   Man in charge of a military unit.

Commodus   Caesar Marcus Aurelius Commodus, AD161–192: Roman Emperor.

Contubernia   Single compartments within barrack blocks: accommodation for 8–10 men and their equipment.

Cornu   Brass instument used to play salutes and coded orders to troops in battle.

Denarius   Silver coin the size of a penny; Roman legionaries were paid 225 a year. It was worth sixteen *asses*. Became worthless in the late third century.

Garum   A popular fish sauce in Roman times.

Gladius   Roman short sword.

Gordanian   Marcus Antonius Gordianus: Roman Emperor in third century.

Haruspices   Soothsayers who interpreted the will of the Gods. The Etrusans were supposed to be better versed in divine things than the Roman augurs; they predicted coming events from the inspection of the entrails of victims slain for that purpose.

Horreum   Granary.

Hypocaust   Underfloor heating; the Roman equivalent of today's central heating.

Imperator   An honorary title confirmed on a general by the Senate; especially after a great victory.

Legate   The officer in command of a legion; a man of senatorial rank.

Legio   The elite regular troops of the Roman Army: legions were some 6,000 strong and contained specialist units of builders.

Legionaries   Soldiers recruited from Roman citizens.

Lictor   Bodyguards to the magistrates; they carried the *fasces* symbolizing the power of the magistrates.

Lituus   Horn used by the army for signalling orders.

Mithraeum   An underground temple built by those who worshipped Mithras.

Milecastle   Small fortlet incorporating gateways to the north and south through the Wall, placed at one Roman mile intervals.

Narrow Wall   Those portions of the Wall finished to a narrower gauge.

Notitia Dignitatum   The *Notitia Dignitatum* derives its name from the description at the beginning of the manuscripts: *Notitia dignitatum omnium tam civilium quam militarium imperii occidentis orientisque*. The document is a list of dignitaries and their areas of responsibility in the Roman Empire about the fourth century.

Numerus   A unit of 200–400 men.

Optio   Second in command to a centurion.

Patrician   A patrician was a person who came from the privileged classes of Rome – the aristocratic families.

Pilum   The Roman spear.

Pliny the Younger   Gaius Plinius Caecilius Secundus, AD61–112: lawyer, author and philosopher. His uncle, Pliny the Elder, died after going to view the eruption of Vesuvius at close quarters on 24 August AD79.

Plebs   The *plebs* were the ordinary people of Rome, as distinguished from slaves. They were distinct from the higher order of patricians.

Praetentura   Front part of a fort between the *via principalis* and the *via praetoria*. The area where the strongest of the cohorts were barracked.

Praetorian Guard   Personal bodyguard and elite force of the Emperor.

Praetorium   Commanding officer's house inside a fort.

Principia   The fort's headquarters, set at its centre.

Scutum   Shield made of two layers of wood laid at right angles to each other.

Seneca   Philosopher, statesman and dramatist, 4BC–AD65. Exiled to Corsica for alleged adultery with Caligula's sister Julia.

Sesterces   The basic Roman monetary unit; in the early Empire the annual salary for an ordinary legionary was 900 *sesterces*.

Stanegate   Roman military road marking the frontier before the building of Hadrian's Wall.

Strigel   A bone, curved scraper used in the bath house for cleaning the skin.

Tacitus   Publius Cornelius Tacitus; senator and historian of the Roman Empire.

Talent   A Greek unit of weight: a talent of silver weighed around 56lb (25.4kg) and was used to distribute large sums of money.

Tepidarium   The warm room in a bath house.

Tertullianus   Quintus Septimius Tertullianus; early Christian author. Coined the word 'trinity'.

Testudo   The famous Roman square formation. Legionaries would form a shield wall all round, while the soldiers in the centre held their *scutum* above their heads. It was also known as the 'tortoise'.

Tribune   A senior staff officer with a legion.

Turf Wall   The section of wall west of the River Irthing at Willowford, originally built in turf rather than stone.

Turret   Small towers built at ⅓-mile (500m) intervals between the milecastles on Hadrian's Wall.

Valetudinarium   Military hospital.

Vallum   First referred to by Bede, the Vallum is the wide flat-bottomed ditch with two earth banks built to the south of the Wall.

Vestal Virgins   The six priestesses of the goddess Vesta, responsible for ensuring that the sacred fire burning in the circular Temple of Vesta never went out.

Vexillum   A small banner (usually red), which was used to denote the commander's position. Also used by detachments serving away from their units.

Via principalis   The main road across a fort.

Vicani   A collective term for civilians living next to a Roman Fort.

Vicus   Civil settlement outside the fort.

Wall-walk   A footpath for troops on the Wall.

BIBLIOGRAPHY

This list does not try to be comprehensive. It does however include all the books used in compiling the present work.

Bidwell, Paul and Hodgson, Nicky, *The Roman Army in Northern England* (2009)

Birley, Anthony, *Hadrian: The Restless Emperor* (1997)

Birley, Eric, *Research on Hadrian's Wall* (1961)

Birley, Robin, *Guide to the Central Sector of Hadrian's Wall* (1963)

Birley, Robin, *The People of Roman Britain* (1979)

Collingwood Bruce, J., *Handbook to the Roman Wall*, 11th edition (1957)

Burton, Anthony, *Hadrian's Wall Path* (2003)

Cassius Dio (trans. Earnest Cary) *Roman History* (9 vols) (1961)

Gibbon, Edward, *The Decline and Fall of the Roman Empire* (6 vols)

Goldsworthy, Adrian, *The Complete Roman Army* (2003)

Heather, Peter, *The Fall of the Roman Empire* (2005)

Hutton, William, *The First Man To Walk Hadrian's Wall* (1802)

Luciana, Roberto, *The Coloseum* (1990)

MacKendrick, Paul, *The Mute Stones Speak: The Story of Archaeology in Italy* (1962)

Pliny (ed. H. Rackham), *Natural History* (1947)

Speller, E., *Following Hadrian* (2002)

Stedman, Henry, *Hadrian's Wall Path* (2006)

Suetonius (trans. Robert Graves), *The Twelve Caesars* (1957)

Virgil (trans. David West), *The Aeneid*

INDEX